ACROSS

1. Hated (8)
5. Elvis film, _ _ _ Las Vegas (4)
7. Wooded hollow (4)
8. Humorous poem (8)
9. Humourous play (6)
12. Covetous (7)
15. Small cucumber (7)
19. Comedian, _ _ _ Clifton (6)
21. Dashing, suave (8)
22. Guzzle (4)
23. Equivalent (4)
24. Go across (8)

DOWN

1. Subtract (6)
2. Edible seed pod (5)
3. US actress, _ _ _ Field (5)
4. Cheek indentation (6)
5. Spoken (6)
6. Foot joints (6)
10. Mud (4)
11. Shadowy (4)
12. Actress, _ _ _ Francis (3)
13. Royal princess (4)
14. Furnace (4)
15. Not Scouts! (6)
16. Detach (6)
17. Strong influence (6)
18. Some _ _ _, Cliff Richard hit of 1987 (6)
19. Rangoon's country (5)
20. Scoundrel (5)

Sea Siders

BASS
COD
CONGEREEL
DOLHIN
GROUPER
HADDOCK
HAKE
HALIBUT
HERRINGS
JELLYFISH
LOBSTER

MACKEREL
MUSSELS
OCTOPUS
OYSTER
PENGUIN
PLAICE
PLANKTON
RAYS
SEAHORSE
SEALS
SEAWEED

SHARK
SHRIMP
SOLE
SQUID
TUNA
TURTLE
WALRUS
WHALES

```
B W S H S H G R S R E T S Y O
G U A H S R A E Y E H P I S Y
C K A L O I A L L T X A Y R S
W R D U R L F E I S B A K G C
K H P T S U E Y A B R W N E N
S E A H O R S E L O U I H O D
R O L L E J E V A L R T T S H
E X L G E U A L E R E K C A M
H O N E Q S W P E P N J D A U
E O B I W F E H E A M D E U S
C M A T H L E B L N O I T Q S
I N S N T P D P V C G L R E E
A I S R U J L F K M C U G H L
L S U P O T C O X O W N I Y S
P T S K N C A P D I U Q S N O
```

ACROSS

1. Brazilian dance (5)
7. Male singer (8)
8. Gleaming (5)
10. Jousting match (10)
12. Infectious viral disease (8)
14. Close by (4)
16. Common weed (4)
17. Knitted jacket (8)
20. Breathtaking (10)
23. Perch (5)
24. Grotesquely carved roof spout (8)
25. Verse [anag] (5)

DOWN

1. Prestige (6)
2. Heavy shoe (4)
3. Twosome (4)
4. Legendary "golden" king (5)
5. Gold coin (9)
6. Shackle (6)
9. *Rockin' All Over the _ _ _,* Status Quo hit (5)
11. Refuge (9)
13. Eggs (3)
15. Bouquet (5)
16. Pattern (6)
18. Vex (6)
19. Poison (5)
21. Unimaginative (4)
22. Painful (4)

Hotel Booking

ASHTRAY	MIRROR
BALCONY	MUSIC
BEDS	NUMBER
CHAIR	PARKING
DESK	PHONE
GLASS	PILLOW
LAMP	POOL
LOCK	REST
LOUNGE	SOAP
MAID	
MANAGER	

```
B  P  S  S  R  P  P  A  O  S
A  E  M  S  W  O  L  L  I  P
L  N  R  A  A  O  R  S  H  O
C  O  E  Y  L  L  D  R  W  N
O  H  S  E  A  E  G  R  I  U
N  P  T  R  B  R  D  I  A  M
Y  C  I  S  U  M  T  A  D  B
M  A  N  A  G  E  R  H  E  E
G  N  I  K  R  A  P  C  S  R
E  G  N  U  O  L  O  C  K  A
```

ACROSS

1. Signalling light (5)
4. Axes (5)
10. Welsh county (5)
11. Gather together (7)
12. Formal ritual (8)
13. Mafia boss (4)
15. Ratify (6)
17. Rajiv _ _ _, Indian PM (6)
19. Purposes (4)
20. Sidewalk (8)
23. Pacify (7)
24. Bobby _ _ _, impressionist (5)
25. Type of owl (5)
26. Overpower (5)

DOWN

2. Look angry (5)
3. Plant used for flavouring (8)
5. Demanding (4)
6. Black and white marked horse (7)
7. Extravaganza (11)
8. German river (5)
9. Organisation (11)
14. Year chart (8)
16. Fragrant flower (7)
18. Imprisoned (5)
21. Star of Love Me Tender (5)
22. Anguish (4)

Artistic

BLAKE

BOTTICELLI

BOUCHER

CEZANNE

CHARDIN

COROT

DALI

DEGAS

DUCHAMP

DUFY

DURER

GAINSBOROUGH

GAUGUIN

GOYA

GRIS

GUARDI

HALS

HOGARTH

MANET

MONET

PICASSO

RAPHAEL

REMBRANDT

ROSA

RUBENS

RYDER

SEURAT

SIGNAC

TITIAN

TURNER

VAN GOGH

VERMEER

WHISTLER

```
G T O R O C C S G R I S W P S
B Y A D A E I L N U E H N I E
L O C H Z P D A L I I D G N T
P T T A G N H H B S D N Y U A
R I N T A U E A T O A R R S
D N C I I T O L E C U N A N O
E U T A A C E R R L E C E H R
G I C R S R E E O R S B H H C
T A U H T S M L R B U A T E S
M E U E A B O E L R S R G I R
S A N G R M E O E I A N D E B
I O N A U M P R A G M R I L D
M K N E R I U G O Y A B A A F
H D Y E T D N H Z U V K G A G
T L V V A N G O G H E D U F Y
```

ACROSS

3. He had a hit song with Daniel (5,4)
8. Consigned (4)
9. Abode (8)
10. Russian currency (6)
13. Milk container (5)
14. Welsh mountain (7)
15. Hound (3)
16. Superficial (7)
17. Money (5)
21. Price-fixing ring (6)
22. Extinct reptile (8)
23. Victuals (4)
24. On edge (9)

DOWN

1. Send to Coventry (9)
2. Introductory (9)
4. Heavily burdened (5)
5. Beginning (7)
6. Jerk (4)
7. *Treasure _ _ _*, TV series (4)
11. Schooling (9)
12. Interval (9)
14. Plant seed (3)
15. Quiescent (7)
18. Loose rock debris (5)
19. Placard (4)
20. Stance (4)

Big Talk

ATHLETIC
BIG
BRAWNY
BURLY
FIRM
HARDY
HEAVY
HUSKY
LUSTY
MANLY
MIGHTY

MUSCULAR
POWERFUL
ROBUST
SINEWY
STOUT
STRAPPING
STRONG
STURDY
TOUGH
VIGOROUS
VIRILE

```
S T S T Y V I G O R O U S
S R M T M H Y L R U B R T
T Y S Y U I O D V N G G R
F U D S S D G I R F B O O
L I K R C B R H Y A B I N
U Y R W U I R L T U H N G
C M L M L T U A S Y B Y N
M I S E A F S T W S U H A
V H S T R A P P I N G E M
U G T E O Y L N A M Y A L
H U W K Y U E U G H U V T
A O I E L W T V I T Y Y A
P T G H Y C I T E L H T A
```

ACROSS

1. Lacking in tact (10)
8. Messiah (7)
9. Type of code (5)
10. Waterless (4)
11. Space (4)
12. Weaken (3)
14. Record album cover (6)
15. Warning fire (6)
18. Trap (3)
20. Former Spanish coin (4)
21. Short skirt (4)
23. Ownership (5)
24. Surgical knife (7)
25. Magnifying instrument (10)

DOWN

1. Bill (7)
2. Portal (4)
3. Religious address (6)
4. Frank Ifield song, *I _ _ _ You* (8)
5. Deserves (5)
6. Murder (11)
7. Accountable (11)
13. Eavesdrop (8)
16. Maim (7)
17. US state, capital Topeka (6)
19. *_ _ _ Frutti,* Little Richard song (5)
22. Saintly aura (4)

Suspense Full

AGENT
BUTLER
CAPER
CASE
CHARACTER
CLUE
CORONER
CRIME
DETECT
DRAMA
FICTION
GUESS

HIDDEN
MONEY
MOTIVE
MURDER
MYSTERY
NOVEL
PATTERN
PLACE
POLICE
PORTRAY
PUZZLE
SLEUTH

SOLVE
STAGE
STORY
SUSPECT
SUSPENSE
SYMBOL
TRAIL
TRAVEL
VICTIM
VILLAIN
WEAPON

```
M F F E B P A C D E D E E D P
I Y N V U L O B M Y S R S W R
T E S I T N E U L C L E A C E
C N U T L H I Y H W E N C M P
I O S O E E G A T S U O B C A
V M P M R R R R L M T R N A C
G U E S S A Y T D L H O T R B
P A N V C H G R T I I C R E E
A D S T E V L O S T D V A Y T
T C E P S U S P C M D I I G H
N R E T T A P I U N E T L S N
N I A S E L F R N Z N M P B O
C M T V A C D I M E Z W W A V
D E M C E E T T G P O L I C E
Y W E N R L P A N O P A E W L
```

ACROSS

1. Spurted (6)
7. A bee-keeper (8)
8. Bird with a large bill (6)
9. Hold (4)
10. *Arsenic and Old _ _ _,* play (4)
12. Modelling material (4)
14. High (4)
16. Investigative reporter, _ _ _ Cook (5)
18. String instrument (5)
21. Play the lead (4)
24. Manage (4)
26. Nocturnal insect (4)
27. Official permit (4)
28. Highest point (6)
29. Soldier (8)
30. Major Italian seaport (6)

DOWN

1. Vacated (3,3)
2. Brief downpour (6)
3. Risk (6)
4. *House of the _ _ _ Sun,* song (6)
5. Indispensable (5)
6. *A _ _ _ in Scarlet,* Sherlock Holmes novel (5)
11. Living (5)
12. Family emblem (5)
13. Alan _ _ _, *"Hawkeye"* actor (4)
15. Singing voice (4)
17. Lubricant (3)
19. Eastern Hemisphere (6)
20. Female warrior (6)
22. Exciting situation (6)
23. Great wealth (6)
24. Snap (5)
25. Prepare for firing (5)

Musical Moments

Circle in the diagram all the words listed below. Then read the leftover letters from left to right, top to bottom, to discover a hidden saying.

ALLEGRO	IINTERPRET	PRESTO
BALANCE	LARGO	SCORE
BASSES	METRONOME	SECTIONS
BASSOONS	MUSICIANS	SIGNALS
BRASS	OBOES	SPEED
CELLOS	OCTAVE	STRINGS
CONCERT	PASSAGE	TROMBONE
CONDUCT	PERCUSSION	TRUMPET
DIRECT	PERFORM	VIOLAS
FLUTES	PHRASING	VIOLIN
GROUP	PIECE	WOODWINDS

```
M C O N D U C T T P B H S E O
S U S C O R E E H B A S S E S
O T S E R P R R P A S S A G E
L S C I M H A P E P S P R E T
L S D U C S T R R E O E B R U
E S R N I I A E C R O E O E L
C T A N I P A T U F N D N B F
E R G L U W I N S O S O L E O
I I A O L O D I S R B D E B R
P N R K N E G O I M E P A D T
T G H S V N G R O N I L O I V
O S W A A I N R N W A G T R E
M P T L M E T R O N O M E E O
T C S A L O I V C A N T R C U
O G R A L T R E C N O C M T S
```

ACROSS

1. Football club, _ _ _ Villa (5)
4. Ire (5)
10. Eagle's nest (5)
11. Cupidity (7)
12. Gem stone (8)
13. Price (4)
15. Rain cloud (6)
17. Creed (6)
19. Join together (4)
20. Beauty product (8)
23. Ground (7)
24. Troubled (5)
25. Edible sea-snail (5)
26. Crowd noise! (5)

DOWN

2. Belt (5)
3. Pass (8)
5. Genuine (4)
6. Capital of Libya (7)
7. Famous name (11)
8. Country, capital Kinshasa (5)
9. Diploma (11)
14. Cocktail wine (8)
16. Ruler (7)
18. Tied (5)
21. Mike _ _ _, heavyweight boxer (5)
22. Sphere (4)

Light Work

AURIOLE
AURORA
BEAM
BRIGHT
BRILLIANT
BUOYANT
DAWN
DAY
DIVINE
EDISON
FEATHERS
FIRE
FLASH
FLOAT

GLIMMER
GLOW
HALO
HELIUM
IGNITE
LAMP
LANTERN
LENS
MATCHES
MOON
MORNING
NOON
PALE
PROJECTOR

RADIATE
RAINBOW
RAY
REFLECT
SHINE
SIGHT
SPECTRUM
STARS
SUNRISE
TELEVISION
TORCH
WEIGHT
WHITE
WINDOW

```
L E T A I D A R O D N E L P P
L A M P S R E H T A E F G W T
M U R T C E P S S T O N O O N
A W I N D O W T T L I L S B A
E L A I H T I O A N G H P N Y
B S S R H S N H R O I B R I O
T O I G O R A O S N L U O A U
N A I R E R M L E R I F J R B
A S G T N O U L F M D U E R S
I T N O O U O A U I W F C E E
L A I N O I S I V E L E T M H
L O T O R N L I I E L I O M C
I T E U E E N G C A H Y R I T
R F A L H E H T P W A A C L A
B R I G H T N W A D Y O H G M
```

ACROSS

1. Way of serving eggs (7)
4. Want (5)
7. Let acre [anag] (7)
8. Cereal crop (5)
9. Spanish currency (6)
12. Painting (8)
15. Immense (8)
17. Barrier (6)
18. Part of a jacket (5)
21. Continent (7)
22. Finicky (5)
23. Varied (7)

DOWN

1. Defer (8)
2. Floor covering (6)
3. Novelist _ _ _ Francis (4)
4. Munch (4)
5. Ex-serviceman (7)
6. Pavilion (4)
10. Stage front (5)
11. Original (5)
13. Tedious (8)
14. Navigation aid (7)
16. Day nursery (6)
18. Baker's product (4)
19. Feminine of Lord (4)
20. Loan (4)

Sporting Life

ARCHERY
ATHLETICS
BADMINTON
BASEBALL
BOWLS
CANOEING
CRICKET
CROQUET
CYCLING
DIVING
FOOTBALL

GLIDING
GOLF
HOCKEY
NETBALL
POLO
RIDING
RUGBY
RUNNING
SAILING
SKIING
SOCCER

SPEEDWAY
SURFING
SWIMMING
TENNIS

```
Q C G N I E O N A C G T Y S M
W R I D I N G L L A B E S A B
B O W L S B B G C Y C L I N G
A Q G J W V N F G A R U G B Y
R U N N I N G D H W F R U F G
C E I K M C T S J D D W O H N
H T L L M X E A K E S E L Y I
E I I P I Z K G R E C C O S F
R Y A L N A C N L P I E P T R
Y E S L G N I I K S T W I D U
E K O A H S R D O T E N N I S
R C G B G D C I P Y L A Q V R
F O O T B A L L I T H S S I Q
T H L E F F M G U Y T D Q N F
Y U F N O T N I M D A B A G A
```

ACROSS

1. Breed of toy terrier (9)
6. Large snake (3)
8. Republic of _ _ _ Rica (5)
9. Church singers (5)
10. Jockey, _ _ _ Scudamore (5)
11. Nuisance (4)
13. Stanza (5)
15. Ransack (5)
17. Indispensable (5)
19. Dig into (5)
21. Folktale (4)
23. Foul (5)
26. Pilfered (5)
27. Fiend (5)
28. Goblin (3)
29. Ship's blade (9)

DOWN

1. Racing boat (5)
2. Book in advance (8)
3. Razor (6)
4. Edge forward (4)
5. Run off to marry (5)
6. A bouncer in cricket (6)
7. Spoilt child (4)
12. Body of water (3)
14. Ultimate (8)
16. Climbing plant (3)
18. Leave alone! (3,3)
20. Likely (6)
21. Sail support (4)
22. Group of monkeys (5)
24. Deride (5)
25. Roman emperor (4)

On the Wing

Can you find the 38 listed British wild birds in the grid?

BITTERN

BLACKBIRD

BUZZARD

COOT

CUCKOO

CURLEW

DIPPER

DUNLIN

DUNNOCK

EIDER

FULMAR

GANNET

GREY
  PLOVER

HERON

HOBBY

JAY

KNOT

LITTLE
  GREBE

MAGPIE

MALLARD

OSPREY

RAVEN

REDSTART

ROBIN

RUFF

SCAUP

SERIN

SHAG

SKYLARK

SMEW

SNIPE

SWALLOW

SWIFT

TEAL

TWITE

WAXWING

WIGEON

WREN

```
N I R E S F U L M A R F F U R
M A G P I E D R I B K C A L B
O D D N E R E V O L P Y E R G
O T R A T S D E R F P W R E N
K F A R M N O E G I W O O B L
C I L O T C E P I N S L A E T
U W L B W G A H S K Y L A R K
C S A I I D G N I W X A W G Q
D W M N T J R R Y K W W Y E K
I E I D E R H A R W G S E L C
P L I A N U J V Z S E H R T O
P R T O N K T E T Z E M P T N
E U P U A C S N O R U Y S I N
R C B X G Y B B O H V B O L U
B I T T E R N N C N I L N U D
```

ACROSS

1. Make ready (7)
5. Portal (4)
9. _ _ _ *For My Sweet,* song (6)
10. Amid (5)
12. Thick-witted (5)
13. Implement (7)
14. Hinder (6)
16. Boil slowly (6)
19. First (7)
21. Monk's attire (5)
23. Sum (5)
24. Picasso painting style (6)
25. Uncommon (4)
26. Preparing for publication (7)

DOWN

2. TV comic actor _ _ _ Atkinson (5)
3. Feign (7)
4. Save (6)
6. Australian marsupial (7)
7. Constancy (10)
8. Step (4)
11. Dispense (10)
15. Hunting dog (7)
17. Occupy (7)
18. Carved (6)
20. Eyot (4)
22. Wide open vessel (5)

Hat's Off

BALACLAVA   MONTERO   STETSON

BEANIE   NIGHTCAP   STRAW

BEAVER   OPERA   SUN

BOATER   PANAMA   TIARA

BONNET   PILLBOX   TIN

BOWLER   PITH   TOPEE

BUSBY   SCARF   TOPPER

CHAPEAU   SNOOD   TURBAN

CLOCHE

COONSKIN

COWBOY

CROWN

DERBY

DUNCE

FEDORA

FELT

FEZ

HARD

HELMET

HOMBURG

HOOD

```
N R R E I N A E B D H W L G Y
I E Y E S T N A R E A T A L F
K M R B T U L A R R A R I G R
S M D R S A H E T E O V R P A
N I T E C U O S F D P U E L C
O K M L R G B B E T B P A R S
O M A W H B O F M M R M O D S
C V M O C N Y G O O A W L T P
A L O B N H C H H N N G E T I
I D O E E O A E A T O T U I L
P J T C W H L P O P S R E N L
E G N B H M R P E O B T I R B
E U O F E E E R N A R A I T O
D Y G T E E A W N C U L G E X
D O O N S Z R P A C T H G I N
```

(crossword grid with numbered cells 1–26)

ACROSS

1. The fool rushed around annoyed (8)
5. Disorderly state of a ship's canteen (4)
8. Direction to stir teas up (4)
9. Reptile found in ground round Persian capital (8)
10. Direct speech (7)
13. Web-footed sailor? (5)
14. They're not national papers, but may be gine out at the pub (5,6)
18. Right sort of life for a shooting man (5)
19. Fascist leader in the red, is brought down (7)
23. He keeps the record of her name, read either way in the catalogue (8)
24. Yearn for ages? (4)
25. Looks for Oriental assent (4)
26. Puts on list making plan seem careless (8)

DOWN

1. He has a craving inside for these beasts (6)
2. Brought down to earth (5)
3. Satisfies fully. Could be an asset (5)
4. Move quickly with a pointed weapon (4)
6. Exit ape takes wrongly to make amends (7)
7. Sent us round at the end of the day (6)
11. Obliterate an article in Irish (5)
12. Sportsman to take a sort of risk out East (5)
13. Treated as per doctor's orders (5)
15. The crime of the accomplice (7)
16. Batsmen make it by running hard, tailors by pressing hard (6)
17. Sayings used in an advertisement for many years (6)
20. Legally preclude poets composing (5)
21. Some sort of spicy hitch? (5)
22. Bird on a string (4)

Ship' Shape

All the words can be followed by 'ship'.

APPRENTICE	HORSEMAN	QUEEN
CENSOR	KING	RELATION
CHAIRMAN	LEADER	SCHOLAR
CITIZEN	MARKSMAN	SEAMAN
COMRADE	MEMBER	TOWN
DICTATOR	OWNER	WORKMAN
FRIEND	PARTNER	
HARD	PENMAN	

```
C W I R T P N I N R J F E
H T O I A A A C W C E R M
A O I R M L E R O T H I A
I N R N K N O I T A L E R
R N E S S M E H P N L N K
M P L O E T A P C E E D S
A S R M E M R N I S A R M
N J B E S E A M A N D I A
G E L H N I T N L E E S N
R N E T A W I L E R R V O
A X I U T R O T A T C I D
E C L K Q I D E L A C H J
E D A R M O C I T I Z E N
```

22

ACROSS

1. Speilberg film, _ _ _ *Park* (8)
5. Incite (4)
7. Chilly (4)
8. Spectator (8)
9. Conflict (6)
12. Ruined city in the Nile (7)
15. Black and white marked horse (7)
19. Building material (6)
21. Engaged (8)
22. Grate (4)
23. Singer, _ _ _ Turner (4)
24. Spray (8)

DOWN

1. Derek _ _ _, star of *I, Claudius* (6)
2. Apportion (5)
3. Fire sign? (5)
4. Sheep-dog (6)
5. Mature (4,2)
6. Innermost skin (6)
10. Sea movement (4)
11. Capital of Peru (4)
12. Mire (3)
13. Birthmark (4)
14. Charter (4)
15. Spend (3,3)
16. White sturgeon (6)
17. Song's words (6)
18. Paper-fastener (6)
19. Apple drink (5)
20. Dimwit (5)

Bathtime

BATH   LATHER   SOAP

BUBBLE   LOOFAH   SPONGE

CLEAN   LOTION   STEAM

COLOGNE   PLUG   SUDS

DOZE   REFRESH   TOWEL

DRAIN   RING   WASH

DRIP   SHAMPOO

HOT   SOAK

```
O H E G N O P S W R I E B
S S E U I I O L E W O T U
I A U E R I S O G W R I B
U W I D W R S H J U E A B
I E O I R D T W N S L W L
O Z I E U A I O E R R P E
E I S S B W I E I U E O J
N I M S T T I N W R F O R
G I A T O E G U K I R P E
O I E L O O F A H W E M H
L I T W R H O E S I S A T
O I S W R S O A P I H H A
C L E A N W R I E U S S L
```

ACROSS

1. Shortcoming (7)
4. Pioneer of television (5)
7. Boorish (7)
8. Bonnie _ _ _, singer (5)
9. Skiing discipline (6)
12. Abandon (8)
15. Identify, pinpoint (8)
17. Criticise severely (6)
18. Erect (5)
21. Hypersensitivity (7)
22. Hazy (5)
23. Long-eared dog (7)

DOWN

1. Ravenous (8)
2. Isolated (6)
3. Downcast (4)
4. Bread actress, Jean _ _ _ (4)
5. Nationality of Mussolini (7)
6. Gloomy (4)
10. Juicy gourd (5)
11. Jeremy _ _ _, British tennis player (5)
13. Outside (8)
14. Sundry (7)
16. Slang talk (6)
18. Explosive sound (4)
19. US frontiersman, _ _ _ Crockett (4)
20. Cry of woe (4)

Musical Term

ADAGIO
ALLEGRO
ALTO
CADENCE
CADENZA
CHANT
CHORAL
CLEF
CODA
CONCERTO
CONTRALTO
DITONE
DOLCE
ETUDE
FANFARE
FINALE
FLAT
FORTE
GAMUT
GLEE
GLIDE
INTERMEZ-
ZO
LARGO
LENTO

MAESTRO
MENO
NOTE
OBBLIGATO
OCTAVE
PIANISSIMO
PICK
PIZZICATO
PRESTO

SCALE
SHARP
SOLO
SONATA
STAFF
TEMPO
TREBLE
TUTTI
VIVO

```
B O T S E R P M E N O E E L G B
F T O O V I V P R O C C T S L O
T L S N T R A I Z T T L N U I T
E A C A D E N Z A E A O H L D N
M S A T G T E Z P D V D J A E E
P I L A E M K I O F E E A R M L
O K E V R C L C C A L L E G R O
N R A E I O F A O N A A P O I L
T L T P Q O F T N F R N T B R O
D N S S R T A O C A O I U B E S
I S A T E U T V E R H F T L C G
T H E H W A S X R E C Y T I N A
O A Z Z C O M R T N A O I G E M
N R E L B E R T O B E S J A D U
E P E O M I S S I N A I P T A T
B F K A R T O T L A R T N O C B
```

ACROSS

1. Muscular (6)
5. Broadway musical & film (4)
7. Proportion (5)
8. Stagger (4)
9. Not any (4)
10. *Goodbye, _ _ _ Jean*, film (5)
11. Required (6)
13. Capital of Latvia (4)
14. Set out (6)
18. Garment (1-5)
21. Continent (4)
22. Quick-witted (6)
24. Throb (5)
25. Conspire (4)
26. Musical starring Chevalier, 1958 (4)
27. Premium bond selector (5)
28. Nourish (4)
29. First oarsman (6)

DOWN

1. Hypodermic needle (7)
2. Lubricated (5)
3. Pulverise (5)
4. Lure (7)
5. Ruler (7)
6. Administrator (7)
12. Sin (3)
15. Franco-German river (7)
16. Converted (7)
17. Slaying (7)
19. The Sun personified (3)
20. Rotary engine (7)
22. Yields (5)
23. Sir Edward _ _ _, English composer (5)

Out Right

All the following words can be linked with the word 'out'.

AND ABOUT

BACK

BALANCE

BLACK

BOARD MOTOR

BREAK

BURST

CLASS

COME

CROP

CROSS

DISTANCE

DRAW

FACE

FIELD

FIGHTING

FLANK

FRONT

GROW

GUESS

LANDISH

LAST

LINE

LOOK

NUMBER

OF BOUNDS

OF DATE

OF POCKET

OF THE WAY

RIGGER

RIGHT

SHINE

SIDE

SPOKEN

STANDING

WEIGH

WORK

F	L	A	N	K	W	O	R	G	M	P	L	A	S	T
R	I	G	G	E	R	E	F	I	G	H	T	I	N	G
O	B	E	I	U	B	E	T	P	L	N	D	P	N	N
N	F	G	L	M	E	U	V	K	O	E	M	O	C	E
T	H	D	U	D	O	S	W	U	C	C	J	R	H	K
C	S	N	A	B	O	O	S	N	E	B	K	C	G	O
S	I	T	A	T	R	O	A	D	O	N	F	E	F	P
C	D	D	A	K	E	L	O	A	C	B	A	T	T	S
L	N	N	O	N	A	C	R	S	U	R	H	A	Z	E
A	A	O	U	B	D	D	N	R	M	E	I	Y	B	C
S	L	R	L	O	M	I	S	A	W	A	X	G	R	A
S	H	A	E	O	B	T	N	A	T	K	N	O	H	F
D	C	I	T	N	H	F	Y	G	C	S	S	S	P	T
K	F	O	N	G	G	K	O	A	M	S	I	Q	T	R
R	R	A	V	E	J	G	B	L	W	A	R	D	Q	W

ACROSS

1. Magician's rod (4)
4. Freshwater fish (5)
7. Set of eight (6)
8. Phobia (4)
9. Cut off (5)
10. Trading place (6)
11. Duty list (4)
12. Premium bond selector (5)
13. Drink of the gods (6)
16. Swift (4)
18. Wine sediment (4)
19. Cling (6)
21. Of the country (5)
22. Immense (4)
24. HMS _ _ _, Charles Darwin's ship (6)
25. Merge (5)
26. Destroy (4)
27. Begin again (6)
28. Vigilant (5)
29. Pipe (4)

DOWN

1. Crisp biscuit (5)
2. Latent (7)
3. Hamper (6)
4. Annoy (6)
5. Income (7)
6. Yoke together (7)
14. Sea-fish (3)
15. Primate (3)
16. List of ingredients (7)
17. Religious rite (7)
18. Young hare (7)
19. Ex-Irish PM, _ _ _ Reynolds (6)
20. Husky (6)
23. Faint trace (5)

Flower Arrangement

ALOE
ALPINE
ARUM
ASPIC
ASTER
AZALEA
BALM
BRIAR
BROOM
BUTTERCUP
CARNATION
CLOVER
CROCUS
DAHLIA
DAISY
FLAG
FOXGLOVE
HENNA
IRIS
JASMINE
LILAC

LILY
LOTUS
LUPIN
MIMOSA
MUSK
MYRTLE
ORCHID
OXLIP
PANSY

POPPY
ROCKET
SEPAL
SUNDEW
TANSY
TULIP
VIOLA
VIOLET
WHIN

```
D J A S M I N E S P I L X O E
K S U M Y S N A T E L O I V L
R A I R B V I O L A P I L U T
Y N L T E K C O R C U O A L R
S E N O I T A N R A C L P M Y
I N F C E P A N S Y R N E P M
A I K A E A M H U B E I S T Y
D P R L E F J O T R T H Z M I
A L N I P U L G O O T W L A O
I A H L S I A A L R U A I S R
L W E D N U S Q G W B E L O C
H U N Y P P C V D L A L Y M H
A C N N I C L O V E R A R I I
D M A C A S T E R B U Z U M D
E V O L G X O F S C M A X T L
```

ACROSS

1. US comedian and actor (3,4)
5. Cringe (5)
8. Pretended (5)
9. Actor, _ _ _ Blessed (5)
10. Mannequin (5)
11. Stamps fastener (5)
13. Praise (5)
14. Snout (4)
17. Spanish currency (6)
19. Up-to-date (6)
22. Fronded plant (4)
24. City in Nebraska, USA (5)
26. Diced (5)
29. Snarl (5)
30. Yellow-red dye (5)
31. Actor/director, _ _ _ Welles (5)
32. Number of wise men (5)
33. Wardrobe assistant (7)

DOWN

1. *On the _ _ _*, Cliff Richard song (5)
2. Conductor's stick (5)
3. Off-cut (7)
4. Mass migration (6)
5. Steel rope (5)
6. Bosun's pipe (7)
7. Curl of hair (7)
12. Anger (3)
15. Imbecile (3)
16. Sin (3)
17. Soothsayer (7)
18. Mechanic's wrench (7)
20. Surround (7)
21. Denotes maiden name (3)
23. Worn away (6)
25. Plant source of tequila (5)
27. Foundation (5)

It's a Deal

AIDE
ALERT
ASK
ASSUME
BASE
BASIC
BEND
CALM
CLARITY
COMMIT-MENT
CONTROL
EFFECTIVE
EGO
EVADE
EXPERT
FACTS
FOCUS
KNOW
LANGUAGE
LOYALTY
MEANING

MONEY
NEED
NEGOTIATE
OBJECTIVE
OPINION
POWER
PRIDE
PRIORITY
SIDE

SLOW
STALL
THEORY
TIME
TONE
VIEW
VISUAL
WANT
WORD

```
B A S I C W E I V I S U A L W
L C L A R I T Y E G C D G A L
A R I R S L L P E N D A N C E
N E N O I N I P O M O T L E H
G W E F G N I N A E M T D M B
U O D A C O M M I T M E N T T
A P I C O L E T A I T O G E N
G D S T G C O N T R O L E H J
E B A S E V A D E E N X C M Y
E V I T C E J B O F P W O C T
P R I O R I T Y T E O N W H L
E M U S S A C G R R E C E T A
E D I R P B C T D Y E O U P Y
J E V I T C E F F E R L C S O
A S K N O W O L S Y S T A L L
```

ACROSS

1. In sight (7)
5. Shut forcibly (4)
7. Nibble (4)
8. Mound of stones (5)
9. _ _ _ Diamond, singer (4)
10. Affair of honour (4)
12. Protection (7)
14. Large bird (6)
18. Spanish cry! (3)
19. Team number (6)
23. Pupil (7)
25. Precious metal (4)
26. Hire vehicle (4)
27. Port in northwest Italy (5)
28. Cairo's river (4)
29. Pass slowly (4)
30. Kentish resort town (7)

DOWN

1. Empty (6)
2. Matelot (6)
3. Package (6)
4. Receded (5)
5. Group of words (8)
6. Fracas (5)
11. River embankment (5)
13. Concern (4)
15. Section (4)
16. Firewood (8)
17. Jimmy _ _ _, radio DJ (5)
20. Accounts book (6)
21. Capital of Austria (6)
22. Nullify (6)
23. Full up (5)
24. Indian pole (5)

Touch Typing

BACK-SPACE   LINE   PRESS

BAR   LOCK   PUSH

BLACK   METAL   SPACE

CASE   NAME   SPOOL

INKS   NUMBER   TABLE

KEYS   PAPER   TABS

LEVER   PORTABLE   TYPE

```
I E U S E C A P S K C A B
I U S A S P A C E I E O E
D R U L Y S T I O N S T O
D R R I E W R B A I E W T
D A I S K V W M S T I E A
B L A C K W E I E I S T B
K C O L W R I R L O O P S
R I E I L W R O B W R I E
E E J N A R E P A P W R S
B L W E T I S W T Q U S I
M B I E E S K W R I E A E
U A W R M S N I O R S T I
N T Y P E I I W P U S H W
```

ACROSS

1. Footballer (10)
8. Conceitedness (7)
9. Lowest point (5)
10. Squalid dwelling (4)
11. Weave (4)
12. Spider's trap (3)
14. Apprehensive (6)
15. Drive away (6)
18. TV bigot, _ _ _ Garnett (3)
20. Smallest particle (4)
21. Clenched hand (4)
23. Adhere to (5)
24. Lower back pain (7)
25. Brotherhood (10)

DOWN

1. Droplet (7)
2. WWII alliance (4)
3. Japanese gown (6)
4. Albert _ _ _, physicist (8)
5. Bequeath (5)
6. Encouragement (11)
7. Severe trial (11)
13. Edible snail (8)
16. Seclusion (7)
17. Tall tree (6)
19. Aviator (5)
22. Zulu regiment (4)

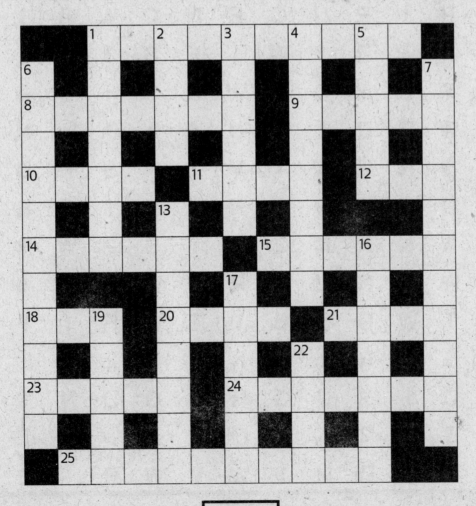

Banking Business

BALANCE	COUNT	SAFE
BONDS	DEBIT	SAVE
BOOK	FAST	SERVE
BORROW	GUARD	TELLER
CASH	LEND	TYPE
CHEQUE	LINES	VAULT
CLERK	LOAN	WINDOW
COST	MONEY	WORK

```
W R I E U Q E H C W R I E
U S W R I W I E S T I L W
S Y E N O M W R S I O E I
D W R R I E U A I A W N S
N S R H W T V I N S F D K
O O S W S E R V E I S E R
B A L A N C E I S P W R E
C W F G U A R D W R Y I L
S T W D E B I T W R I T C
E S W R I O K T E L L E R
N O I S O O R C O U N T I
I C W R I K O E A W R I E
L W O D N I W V W R I E S
```

ACROSS

1. Safeguard (7)
5. Nourish (4)
9. Continent (6)
10. Roman soothsayer (5)
12. Larceny (5)
13. Vocation (7)
14. Hullabaloo (6)
16. Very recent (3-3)
19. Permitted (7)
21. Chronic drinker (5)
23. Confess (3,2)
24. Concurred (6)
25. Finished level (4)
26. Worship (7)

DOWN

2. Awaken (5)
3. Family name in *Only Fools and Horses* (7)
4. Grip tightly (6)
6. European language (7)
7. Uncomplimentary (10)
8. Surety money (4)
11. Fortress (10)
15. Apprentice (7)
17. Hold spellbound (7)
18. Actor, _ _ _ Fox (6)
20. Variety (4)
22. Crush (5)

Tribal

ALEUT

APACHE

ARAPAHO

ARIKAREE

AZTEC

CARIB

CATAWBA

CAYUGA

CHEROKEE

CHEYENNE

CHINOOK

CHOCTAW

COMANCHE

CREE

CROW

FOX

HOPI

INCA

IROQUOIS

KICKAPOO

KIOWA

MAYA

MICMAC

MOHAWK

MOHICAN

OJIBWAY

ONEIDA

OSAGE

PAWNEE

PONCA

PUEBLO

SAUK

SEMINOLE

SENECA

SHAWNEE

SHOSHONE

SIOUX

SNAKE

TETON

ZUNI

```
N N A R I K A R E E Z N A O E
Y X U O I S N E W P U K R O H
A O S O A O R O E E N W A P C
W F W E T C R N E G I A P A N
B A A E N C N K M A R H A K A
I R T R R E O I O S R O H C M
J P C B Y R C A B O N M O I O
O O O E E M P A Y E N S D K C
D N H H A A D U I A T I S N A
C C C C C C C D E U M O H A B
E A G H A A A K E B G U A C W
T J E Y R J S L U J L Q W I A
Z K U I E K A N S A K O N H T
A G B E L O N I M E S R E O A
A E N O H S O H S V V I E M C
```

ACROSS

1. Black treacle (8)
5. Travelling show (4)
7. Completed (4)
8. Spirited (8)
9. Hot and humid (6)
12. The Hebrew God (7)
15. Artillery emplacement (7)
19. Musical piece by Ravel (6)
21. Aversion (8)
22. Motor-racing servicing area (4)
23. Horse's colouring (4)
24. Ron _ _ _, football manager (8)

DOWN

1. One of the three Gorgons (6)
2. Representative (5)
3. Hair-raising (5)
4. Smother (6)
5. Spanish dictator (6)
6. Salad plant (6)
10. Pillage (4)
11. Widespread (4)
12. Peter _ _ _, BBC economics reporter (3)
13. Tramp (4)
14. Despicable (4)
15. Margin (6)
16. Minor Greek sea-god (6)
17. Former Soviet republic (6)
18. Linda _ _ _, *Birds of a Feather* actress (6)
19. Shatter (5)
20. Tall flower (5)

Countywise

Find all the listed places in Cumbria, starting from the letter K, move up, down, left or right; (not diagonally), making a continuous trail. The last item (not listed) is a Cumbrian lake.

AMBLESIDE

APPLEBY

BARROW-IN-FURNESS

BRAMPTON

BRIGHAM

CARLISLE

COCKER-MOUTH

CONISTON

ESKDALE GREEN

GRASMERE

HAWK-SHEAD

KENDAL

KESWICK

MARYPORT

PENRITH

SEATON

SHAP

SILECROFT

SILLOTH

TEBAY

THURSBY

ULVERSTON

WHITEHAVEN

WIGTON

WINDERMERE

WORKINGTON

```
P T O L E S E U I S L H A V E
M W N B M I D L L W E E I W N
A I G T A R E V R H I T N D E
R B N O N S N S A C N R E M R
M H E E O T O E A T O E T E B
A A W R N G T R R A E R E M A
H G K G W N I O W B T R A S Y
R I S E O R K N I Y H G Y B A
B E H L A D K F U B U I S E P
T A D E S K E N R S R N T L P
F C E C I W S E S S C O O N S
O R L K E R R O P Y R A A D I
I T I C K M T R W E N M L N L
R H S O C O S E D W T R K E L
N E P H T U H A P A T E H T O
```

ACROSS

1. Strike (5)
4. Pinch (5)
10. Sleepy (5)
11. Jeopardise (7)
12. Wolverhampton Wanderers' football ground (8)
13. Unite (4)
15. Sumptuous (6)
17. Small drum (3-3)
19. School period (4)
20. Illicit (8)
23. Whinnied (7)
24. The Confederate states of America (5)
25. Actor, _ _ _ Lundgren (5)
26. A newly-wed (5)

DOWN

2. Ethical (5)
3. Neatness (8)
5. Sobbed (4)
6. Aviation terminal (7)
7. Exhilarating (11)
8. Less (5)
9. Famous US bandleader (5,6)
14. Perfumed ball (8)
16. Dizziness (7)
18. Positive electrode (5)
21. Mended (5)
22. Hew (4)

...The Ball

BLOCK   HOLD   SHOOT

BOUNCE   INFLATE   SLAM

CATCH   KICK   SPIKE

DRIBBLE   PASS   STOP

DROP   PITCH   THROW

DUNK   PUNT   VOLLEY

HEAD   ROLL

HIT   SERVE

```
D J N B O U N C E A U I Z
K R O T Q I J V L S O M B
C Y I O E R V E K I P S Y
I H U B E Q X C I N O L E
N P O N B B O H C F U P L
F P O M A L S U K M Y D L
L N T R B D E R W N O T O
A O L O D V V O C H I M V
T B Y L O P R J P U D X P
E N O L M H E A D I L O I
Q H U R T P S W O Y T N A
C J V P N S D R U S J C D
X O U B N C Y H C T A C H
```

ACROSS

1. Obstinate (6)
5. Beer flavouring (4)
7. Christopher _ _ _, *Superman* actor (5)
8. Lasso (4)
9. Poker stake (4)
10. Vigilant (5)
11. Climb (6)
13. Part of a shoe (4)
14. Salad plant (6)
18. Malayan jungle knife (6)
21. Dread (4)
22. Public procession (6)
24. *Pygmalion* character, _ _ _ Doolittle (5)
25. Swimming competition (4)
26. Wooded hollow (4)
27. US actress, _ _ _ Close (5)
28. Smoke outlet (4)
29. Sikh's headdress (6)

DOWN

1. Inactive (7)
2. Farmyard birds (5)
3. Apprehension (5)
4. Grow (7)
5. US actress, _ _ _ Locklear (7)
6. Design (7)
12. Snare (3)
15. Comprehensive (7)
16. Amount of land (7)
17. Policeman (7)
19. Turkish lord (3)
20. Troublesome sprite (7)
22. Rolling Stones hit, _ _ _ *It Black* (5)
23. Horseman (5)

Bone Idle

ANKLE	FISH	RIBS
BACK	HEAD	SKULL
BREAST	HEEL	SPINE
CHEEK	MARROW	ULNA
CHINA	MEAL	WHALE
COLLAR	NASAL	WISH
FEMUR	NECK	WRIST

```
K C E N B R E L A H W B F
N P N V P K S R N N C L G
W N I F F P L B L S O N F
D I P L A E M F U P L L B
F S S B E P J U F H L B R
W L L H W B A F L H A T N
O J F P B R N N J C R R Q
R B J K E E H C K R J M T
R I F L H A B T L L U K S
A H B A R S M V J H E N I
M S K S F T I L F E M U R
T F C A H F N F L A F R W
R Y A N I H C B N D F N R
```

ACROSS

1. Obstinate (6)
5. Beer flavouring (4)
7. Christopher _ _ _, *Superman* actor (5)
8. Lasso (4)
9. Poker stake (4)
10. Vigilant (5)
11. Climb (6)
13. Part of a shoe (4)
14. Salad plant (6)
18. Malayan jungle knife (6)
21. Dread (4)
22. Public procession (6)
24. *Pygmalion* character, _ _ _ Doolittle (5)
25. Swimming competition (4)
26. Wooded hollow (4)
27. US actress, _ _ _ Close (5)
28. Smoke outlet (4)
29. Sikh's headdress (6)

DOWN

1. Inactive (7)
2. Farmyard birds (5)
3. Apprehension (5)
4. Grow (7)
5. US actress, _ _ _ Locklear (7)
6. Design (7)
12. Snare (3)
15. Comprehensive (7)
16. Amount of land (7)
17. Policeman (7)
19. Turkish lord (3)
20. Troublesome sprite (7)
22. Rolling Stones hit, _ _ _ *It Black* (5)
23. Horseman (5)

You Can Talk!

ARGUE   MENTION   SPEECH

AVER   MUTTER   TALK

BABBLE   PRATE   TATTLE

BANTER   PRATTLE   TERSE

BLAB   QUOTE   WARBLE

BLURT   RAVE   WORD

DRONE   RELATE

JOKE   SHRIEK

```
Q T E T A L E R V E N D P
P A R F M R L F V S R R V
W T H E L B B A B F A O V
G T N L B R R B H T C N T
K L A T J J A H E S R E T
X E N T N L W J Q P M R F
J J F A B D B W S U T F B
S T V R L B O P T V O T H
T E F P G R E T N A B T C
R M E T D R E F B R B N E
U T K E I R H S R G T S E
L B O L Y X R F Z U B F P
B B J V N O I T N E M F S
```

ACROSS

1. Speak softly (7)
5. Carrion bird (4)
9. Punctual (6)
10. Colorado ski resort (5)
12. Cartridge (5)
13. Lull (7)
14. Tainted (6)
16. Devastation (6)
19. Blood disorder (7)
21. Sow (5)
23. Jeremy _ _ _, actor (5)
24. Sailor's song (6)
25. Grand Prix driver, _ _ _ Lauda (4)
26. Forecast (7)

DOWN

2. *A Man called* _ _ _, film (5)
3. Alike (7)
4. Whole (6)
6. Copy (7)
7. Night-clothes fabric (10)
8. The Red Planet (4)
11. Assessment (10)
15. Male peafowl (7)
17. Clap (7)
18. Sid _ _ _, US comedian/actor (6)
20. Disguise (4)
22. Garret (5)

It's a Synonym

You will not find the words listed below in the diagram. Instead, you will be looking for synonyms of these words. For example, instead of AWKWARD, you will find CLUMSY.

AWKWARD

BABBLE

BOGUS

BOTHER

CLAW

DEMONSTRATE

EXERTION

GAINSAY

GOVERN

ILLUSION

JUST

MIND

PRICE

PROBABLE

PUPIL

REBUKE

SILENCE

TIRESOME

TITULAR

VICTORY

```
A E F F O R T A M A H S
C I H C S B C H N T Y D
U O O U H O F D N N J D
P L N D S I F E U Y O F
R Y O T F H D C L L C Y
I S R G R U B E G O L F
G M A V T A K P N D T J
H U R S C I D T G N K S
T L Y F L T R I U M P H
A C T A L O N O C H D O
T C E L L E T N I T D W
Q F N C H A T T E R I K
```

ACROSS

6. Highborn (12)
8. Mixture (7)
9. Girl's name (5)
10. Old Ireland (4)
12. Delicate (6)
14. Danger (5)
15. Hire charge (6)
16. German river (4)
19. Herring-like fish (5)
21. Pariah (7)
22. TV quiz, hosted by Henry Kelly (5,3,4)

DOWN

1. Neurotic Obsession (8)
2. Platform (5)
3. Scallywag (5)
4. Lumber factory (3-4)
5. Fruit skin (4)
6. Unprofessional (10)
7. Lacking body fluids (10)
11. Actor, _ _ _ Gibson (3)
12. Coniferous tree (3)
13. Peacemaker (8)
14. Departure (7)
17. Disney dog (5)
18. Tempest (5)
20. Run wild (4)

Bone Idle

ANKLE   FISH   RIBS

BACK   HEAD   SKULL

BREAST   HEEL   SPINE

CHEEK   MARROW   ULNA

CHINA   MEAL   WHALE

COLLAR   NASAL   WISH

FEMUR   NECK   WRIST

```
K C E N B R E L A H W B F
N P N V P K S R N N C L G
W N I F F P L B L S O N F
D I P L A E M F U P L L B
F S S B E P J U F H L B R
W L L H W B A F L H A T N
O J F P B R N N J C R R Q
R B J K E E H C K R J M T
R I F L H A B T L L U K S
A H B A R S M V J H E N I
M S K S F T I L F E M U R
T F C A H F N F L A F R W
R Y A N I H C B N D F N R
```

ACROSS

1. Flashy (6)
5. Cover (3)
7. Peri (5)
8. *The _ _ _*, Tony Hancock film (5)
9. Olympic competitor (7)
13. Christen (4)
14. Midlands river (5)
17. Roll of parchment (6)
18. In condition (3)
19. Vitality (6)
20. Incantation (5)
23. Whirlpool (4)
25. Baby's outfit of clothes (7)
28. Female relative (5)
29. Foyer (5)
30. Neckband (3)
31. Turn up (6)

DOWN

1. Castle tower (6)
2. Quiver (6)
3. Show mercy (6)
4. Yearning (4)
5. Ancient harp (4)
6. Palm fruit (4)
7. Froth (4)
10. Try (4)
11. Conifer (5)
12. Hooked claw (5)
15. Mikhail Gorbachev's wife (5)
16. Loose loop (5)
18. Worry (4)
20. Young swan (6)
21. Building extension (6)
22. Cotton (6)
24. Moist (4)
25. Bequeathed (4)
26. American university (4)
27. Cylinder (4)

Jest a Minute

BANTER
BRILLIANT
BUFFOON
CHUCKLE
CLEVER
CLOWN
COMEDY
CORNY
CUT-UP
DROLL
FOOL
FUNNY
GAG
GIGGLE
HILARIOUS
HORSEPLAY
JEST
JOCOSE
JOKE
JOLLY
JOSH
KEEN
KIDDING
LAUGH

MERRY
PLAY
PRANK
PUN
QUICK
QUIP
RAZZ
SATIRE
SHARP

SPORT
SURPRISE
TEASE
TRICK
WHIMSEY
WISECRACK
WIT
WORDPLAY
ZANY

```
G A G U T R O P S Y O W E Y S
A J Y N O N U R D R O L L A O
H O E M I N A E U R E V E L C
N G U S H D M I D S H A R P B
U U U S T O D P L P I U Q E U
Z I O A C R L I Y L A U P S F
A J K T L A I N K L I N T R F
N E N I Y C J C E C B R F O O
Y S A R T O A N K L A U B H O
E A R E L R F O O L N O P P N
S E P L C N U R J N T I W U U
M T Y E W Y L E Y K E E N T P
I E S O C O J E S I R P R U S
H I L A R I O U S Z Z A R C H
W C H U C K L E L G G I G R O
```

ACROSS

1. Brave woman? (5)
4. Plural of that (5)
10. Utilising (5)
11. Suffering (7)
12. Conspiracy (8)
13. Opera singer, _ _ _ Te Kenawa (4)
15. Human (6)
17. Wooded area (6)
19. Domesticated (4)
20. Elongate (8)
23. British instrumental group (7)
24. Singer, _ _ _ Stardust (5)
25. Actress, Dame _ _ _ Ashcroft (5)
26. Orderly pile (5)

DOWN

2. Bed-cover (5)
3. Church of England (8)
5. Immense (4)
6. Hara-kiri (7)
7. Coin collector (11)
8. Politician, William _ _ _ (5)
9. Baptism (11)
14. Moving (8)
16. Ransack (7)
18. Intellectual society (5)
21. Chaos (5)
22. Ballad (4)

Round & Round

BANDAGE

BELT

BRACE

BRAID

CINCH

CINCTURE

CIRCLE

CIRCUIT

CIRCUM-
FERENCE

CORDON

FERRULE

FILLET

GIRTH

HOOP

LATITUDE

LINE

MERIDIAN

ORBIT

RIBAND

RIBBON

RING

SASH

SCARF

STRAP

STRIP

SURCINGLE

TAPE

TWINE

TWIST

WITHE

WRIST-BAND

ZODIAC

ZONE

```
E G A D N A B F H P I R T S W
L L K I Y G E R U T C N I C D
G E C H T R I G D D G E I A Z
N P K R R G Z S N J N R F R T
I A D U I I J A D I C F T F H
C T L J T C B H L U R W I K M
R E N G T I J B M Z I C B E D
U L J O R L U F O S E A R L N
S L O A D S E C T N J I O U A
B I H H F R T B R G D D V N B
J F R C E E O R F I I O J O T
Z S Z N H N F C A A C Z F Z S
O K C I J I K N R P O O H A I
N E D C G W G B R A C E S F R
E D U T I T A L J G E H T I W
```

ACROSS

1. US inventor, _ _ _ Colt (6)
7. Short story (8)
8. Jog one's memory (6)
9. Love excessively (4)
10. One of the apostles (4)
12. Track (4)
14. Ardent (4)
16. Majestic (5)
18. Glowing coal (5)
21. Head cook (4)
24. US female singer (4)
26. On the sheltered side (4)
27. *Ride a White _ _ _*, T.Rex song (4)
28. Popular instrument (6)
29. Contradict (8)
30. Sour (6)

DOWN

1. Whoop (6)
2. Mutter (6)
3. Stockings flaw (6)
4. Church room (6)
5. Capital of Bulgaria (5)
6. Juicy fruit (5)
11. Below (5)
12. Location (5)
13. Inflection (4)
15. Engrave (4)
17. Poem (3)
19. Word of caution (6)
20. Forest warden (6)
22. Frenzied (6)
23. Flowery (6)
24. Unrefined (5)
25. Live (5)

Home from Home

ATTIC
BATH
BOOKCASE
CARPET
CELLAR
CHAIRS
CLOCK
CUPBOARD
CUSHION
CUTLERY
DOORS
FIRE
FLAT
FLOOR
HALLWAY
IRON
KITCHEN
LAMP
LIGHT
LIVING
  ROOM
LOUNGE

PICTURE
PANS
POTS
PLANTS
RADIO
ROOF
ROOMS
SINK
SOFA

STAIRS
TABLE
TELEPHONE
TELEVISION
TOILET
VASE
WALLS
WARDROBE
WINDOWS

```
C A E T H G I L Y R E L T U C
E S F R N O I S I V E L E T R
L R J O U S R I A H C L N O K
L I P O S T R P F S B M E I Q
A A M F G O C S A A T O H L T
R T A D N H R I T N E O C E E
E S L I P O T S P H S R T T L
Y E B O O K C A S E A G I D E
A B S D K N I S B P V N K R P
W O M C E T S W O D N I W A H
L R O F E R C L O C K V L O O
L D O P L N I A R A D I O B N
A R R O B A T F R O O L F P E
H A P L A N T S N O I H S U C
C W A L L S A E G N U O L C M
```

ACROSS

1. Extremely bad (7)
5. Ken _ _ _, comedian (4)
9. Channel (6)
10. _ _ _ Island, former US Immigration Centre (5)
12. Austrian composer, Franz Joseph _ _ _ (5)
13. Old-fashioned (7)
14. Joan _ _ _, US comedienne (6)
16. Happy cries! (6)
19. Lacking consistency (7)
21. Edwin _ _ _, Motown singer (5)
23. Leather strap (5)
24. Powerless (6)
25. Prying (4)
26. Pupil (7)

DOWN

2. Cartoon character _ _ _ Boop (5)
3. William _ _ _, *Star Trek* actor (7)
4. Of the stars (6)
6. Askew (7)
7. Pharmacy (10)
8. Warmth (4)
11. Popular dance of the twenties (10)
15. Several (7)
17. Spouse (7)
18. Absolve (6)
20. Best clothes! (4)
22. Cricketer, _ _ _ Lamb (3)

Island Hopping

AMOY
ARUBA
AZORES
BAHAMAS
BALI
BERMUDA
BIKINI
BORNEO
CANARY
CAPRI
CAYMAN
CELEBES
CHANNEL
CHRISTMAS
CORFU
CRETE
CYPRUS
EASTER
FALKLANDS
FIJI
GRENADA
GUAM
JAVA
KISKA
KODIAK

MALDIVE
MIDWAY
PALAU
PANAY
PITCAIRN
RHODES
SAIPAN
SAMOA
SARK

SICILY
SOCIETY
SUMATRA
TAHITI
TARAWA
TIMOR
TONGA
VIRGIN
WAKE

```
S E B E L E C N I G R I V J S
S U R P Y C A V A J Y O M A A
E F M I D W A Y E N L F D B M
R R I A A O A T A E I A R U T
O O L R T P E M N J N L O R S
Z C A N A R Y N I E I K M A I
A T B K C A A L R S K L I K R
I R P A C H N G I O I A T N H
T E A I C S A R K C B N G S C
I V A D T E P R S I I D U U S
H I G O U C Y W E E S S A A A
A D N K B M A L B T D K M L I
T L O C D K R I Y Y S O A A P
S A T G E G G E R N A A H P A
T M S A M A H A B N V W E R N
```

ACROSS

1. Roberta _ _ _, US singer (5)
4. Milk container (5)
10. Actress, _ _ _ Streep (5)
11. Wash and iron (7)
12. *From Here to _ _ _*, book and film title (8)
13. Hairless (4)
15. Story in parts (6)
17. Ordained minister (6)
19. Pop singer, _ _ _ Kamen (4)
20. Specially trained soldier (8)
23. Sightseer (7)
24. Heather genus (5)
25. Dessert (5)
26. Chamfered edge (5)

DOWN

2. Peter _ _ _, hooded-eyed US actor (5)
3. Year chart (8)
5. Drag (4)
6. Needless bureaucracy (3,4)
7. Mimic (11)
8. Popeye's arch enemy! (5)
9. Style of jazz (11)
14. First showing (8)
16. Hermit (7)
18. Tall (5)
21. Din (5)
22. Tablet (4)

Book Marked

ADVENTURE
AUTHOR
BOOKS
CHAPTERS
COVER
DETECTIVE
EDITION
EPIC
FABLE
FICTION
GOAL
GOTHIC
HERO
HISTORICAL
HOPE
LEGEND
LOVE
MYSTERY
PAGES
PAPER-
BACK
PLOT
PROSE

PUBLISH
READER
ROMANCE
SAGA
SCARY
SCI-FI
SEQUEL
SERIES
SORT

STORY
SUSPENSE
TALE
TELL
TYPE
WESTERN
WHODUNIT
WORDS
WRITERS

```
X Y P S R E T I R W S A G A E
S R O D P S L O V E G L D P S
E A W R T E H M N B D V E A N
R C O O E T D H O P E A T P E
I S R W U H G I I N P Q E E P
E Y L A C I R O T S I H C R S
S R W D W N L U C I C U T B U
M E E N O H R H I B O Q I A S
H T S E S E O E F O L N V C R
U S T G K L M D T T Y P E K E
M Y I E O B A G U S N R I P T
R M L L O A N O T N E F V O P
R A L X B F C A R V I W H L A
T E S E Q U E L O C L T O K H
T Z S E G A P C S G O T H I C
```

Just a cryptic crossword

ACROSS

1. Shows entertainment in a Norfolk town (8)
5. Look, turn round and look again (4)
8. Emotional state caused by a reversal of fate (4)
9. Wind power? (3,5)
10. Calls for superior judgement (7)
13. River you might find her in (5)
14. Motorists hope that they don't fall off in the autumn (4,7)
18. Mineral found by artist in the receptacle (5)
19. Give back to the Sappers depot (7)
23. They transport vehicles round heartless river (8)
24. Bail out in the Indian Ocean (4)
25. To be generous, hand over a few (4)
26. Disc of the month (4,4)

DOWN

1. It's humiliating to do this to oneself (6)
2. Company involved in a soaking? Bail out (5)
3. To be of value or service when Miss Gardner reached 49 (5)
4. Certain kind of ruse (4)
6. Making a mistake about a piece of jewellery (3-4)
7. Looked like a lord? (6)
11. Add to FIFA XI that is reshuffled when they lose a player (5)
12. Excellent purse ruined (5)
13. Hand brakes of a sort! (5)
15. Listener guest involved in a murder (7)
16. It counted a hundred in a vehicle (6)
17. Military unit has private soldier captured in Christmas rising (6)
20. Supporter of the art world (5)
21. Game amongst the ducks in New Zealand (5)
22. Both sides of the paper (4)

Weather Report

ATMOSPHERE
BREEZE
BRIGHT
CHILLY
CLOUDS
COLD
CYCLONE
DEPRESSION
DROUGHT
DRY
DULL
EASTERLY
FOG
FREEZING
GALE
HAIL
HEATWAVE
HOT
HUMID
ICE
MILD

MISTY
NORTHERLY
PRESSURE
RAINY
SEASONAL
SNOW
SOUTHERLY
STORMY

SULTRY
SUNNY
TEMPERATURE
WARM
WEATHER
WESTERLY
WET
WINDY

```
C H I L L Y Y L R E T S E W E
L U O T L D R Y S E M L I A H
O L D T N U E T M T H G I R B
U G H I S T D P L Y O T N M S
D N W T E W E M L U F T A C D
S I E C V R P R E S S U R E R
O Z I U A P E Z E E R B P E W
U E D T W H T H G U O R D D C
T E U M T U D O P I E F S L Y
H R E R A M P R Y S G T N I C
E F O S E I T A S N O G I M L
R N O M H D W I N R N M A G O
L R H G P I O N M U S U T L N
Y T S I M N N Y L R E T S A E
N E L A N O S A E S B D L O C
```

ACROSS

1. Journey (6)
4. Cricket bat wood (6)
7. Idi _ _ _, Ugandan despot (4)
8. Quarter-pint measure (4)
9. Dialogue (6)
11. Mushrooms, toadstools etc. (5)
12. Ribbon (4)
14. Hollywood star, _ _ _ Garbo (5)
16. Trap (5)
18. Country in SE Asia (5)
20. Freshwater fish (5)
21. Black _ _ _, Dick Turpin's horse (4)
23. Form of oxygen (5)
25. Fisherman (6)
28. New Zealander (4)
29. Silage container (4)
30. _ _ _ Zhivago, Pasternak novel (6)
31. Parlour (6)

DOWN

1. Vehicles (7)
2. Line up (5)
3. Coil (4)
4. Donned (4)
5. Illumination (5)
6. Kim _ _ _, Kids in America singer (5)
9. Vision (5)
10. Everlasting (7)
13. Tennis player, _ _ _ Shriver (3)
15. Detest (5)
17. Beer (3)
19. Frightening (7)
21. Parched (5)
22. Canonised person (5)
24. Pungent bulb (5)
26. Equipment (4)
27. Wickedness (4)

Elementary

ATOM
BORON
ELEMENT
FERMIUM
FLUORINE
GAS
GOLD
HELIUM
HYDROGEN
INDIUM
IODINE
IRON
KRYPTON
LEAD
LITHIUM
MAGNE-
  SIUM
MELT
MERCURY
METAL
MIX

NEON
NICKEL
NITROGEN
ORE
OXYGEN
PART
PHOSPHORUS
PLATINUM

RADIUM
RADON
SILICON
SILVER
SODIUM
TIN
XENON
ZINC

```
T T L E K C I N O T P Y R K M
N L G A S U R O H P S O H P U
E E S U L F F R T Z I N C N U
M M N E N I D O I T N R I K I
E R E E R L T R N E A T O M N
L M O R O A S H G T R A P N F
E N A G C I D Y I O P H U L A
L P J G L U X I G U Y O U D H
A B M V N O R E U D M O R A H
L O E U M E N Y R M R T G E K
L R T B I H S O M I X V L L T
I O A S C M G I N O C I L I S
U N L B W E R E U M U I D N I
M J N O N E X E B M U I D O S
P L A T I N U M F D N O D A R
```

ACROSS

1. Sir Walter _ _ _, British explorer (7)
7. Object d'art (5)
8. Doncaster horse race (2,5)
9. Stanley _ _ _, Scottish impersonator (6)
11. Edible entrails (5)
13. Bishop of Rome (4)
14. Two-pack card game (7)
15. Spouse (4)
16. Fundamental (5)
17. Outmoded (3,3)
21. Shortage (7)
22. Mixed cold dish (5)
23. *The Towering* _ _ _, disaster movie (7)

DOWN

2. Simulated (10)
3. Gracefulness (8)
4. *Duty Free* actress, _ _ _ Taylor (4)
5. Mountain lion (4)
6. Sieve (4)
9. Explode (5)
10. Safari (10)
12. Out of condition (5)
13. Garden of Eden (8)
18. Cart (4)
19. Moor (4)
20. Gaunt (4)

Flying Visit

AIR HOSTESS

AIRPORT

ALTIMETER

CABIN

CLUB CLASS

COCKPIT

CONTROL TOWER

CONTROLS

DUTY/FREE

FILM

FIRST
  CLASS

FLIGHT

FUSELAGE

HOLIDAYS

LANDING

LIFE/
  JACKET

MEALS

OXYGEN/
  MASK

PILOT

SIGNS

STEWARD

TAIL

TAKE OFF

TAXI

TRIPS

UNDERCARRIAGE

WINDOWS

WINGS

```
C E G A I R R A C R E D N U S
V O B S T T R O P R I A K W C
M J C A P S G D H C P S O L R
F L I K R G M O F C A D U X E
G L I H P N L I O M N B F P T
E Z I F K I L N I I C X I Y E
G S T G D W T X W L O L R N M
A W T A H R A T A X O T S G I
L V Y E O T A S Y T E L T N T
E S E L W K S G K K A R C I L
S Y S E E A E G C E I C L D A
U L N O R N R A M P Q U A N Y
F I F G Y F J D S I G N S A T
M F S S E T S O H R I A S L U
J E R E W O T L O R T N O C D
```

ACROSS

1. Ridiculous (7)
5. Military base (4)
7. Milky gemstone (4)
8. Muslim religion (5)
9. Dry and dusty (4)
10. Elderly (4)
12. North of England city (4)
13. University award (6)
17. Ballet skirt (4)
18. Hawaiian garland (3)
19. Shelley _ _ _, *Cheers* actress (4)
20. Higher-ranking (6)
24. Brainwave (4)
26. Actress, _ _ _ Tushingham (4)
27. Wound dressing (4)
28. Aplomb (5)
29. US stunt motorcyclist, _ _ _ Knievel (4)
30. Tote (4)
31. Ugly sight (7)

DOWN

1. Ally (6)
2. Rectangular (6)
3. Resident (6)
4. _ _ _, *I Shrunk the Kids,* film (5)
5. Drifting micro-organisms (8)
6. Small dagger (8)
11. Girl's name (5)
14. Rid of evil spirits (8)
15. Names book (8)
16. Young eel (5)
21. Pass by (6)
22. Bluish dye (6)
23. Paul _ _ _, US Revolutionary hero (6)
25. Passageway (5)

Postbag

ADDRESS

BAG

BOX

CARTON

COLLECT

CORD

CORRESPOND

COUNTRY

DELIVERY

ENVELOPE

EXPRESS

FRAGILE

LABEL

LETTER

MESSAGE

NAME

NOTE

OPEN

PACKET

PAPER

PARCEL

PEN PAL

POSTCARD

POSTCODE

POSTMAN

RECORDED

ROYAL MAIL

SACK

SEAL

SEND

SIGN

SORT

STAMP

STRING

TAPE

TOWN

VAN

WEIGH

WRAP

WRITE

```
L E B A L D R E P O L E V N E
E W P P U M L I A M L A Y O R
L L O S S E R D D A Q P A R W
I E S B O S S D E D R O C E R
G C T T P S E A L T N E P A T
A R C P N A C C R A G G D E E
R A O O W G P O M W I N R X N
F P D S O E S E R A S I A O Y
N L E T T E R I R D F R C B R
O P T M C V T G T N N T T L E
T M O A A E X P R E S S S A V
R A N N H M L J K S K K O P I
A T W E I G H L L C B C P N L
C S I Y R T N U O C A A A E E
D N O P S E R R O C V S G P D
```

ACROSS

1. Small fowl (6)
4. *The Day of the _ _ _*, film (6)
7. Rise sharply (4)
8. Floppy (4)
10. Part of a bridle (5)
11. Shimmer (7)
14. Golf peg (3)
15. Symbol (5)
17. Claptrap! (5)
18. Actress, _ _ _ Sheridan (5)
19. Brim (3)
21. Eminent musician (7)
24. Greek island (5)
26. Emporium (4)
28. Earth satellite (4)
29. Canned (6)
30. Continue (6)

DOWN

1. Pannier (6)
2. Toss (5)
3. Italian city (5)
4. Fruit preserve (3)
5. *The Bridge on the River _ _ _*, film (4)
6. Slacken (6)
9. Excuse (7)
11. Black and white sea-bird (4)
12. Connecting strip of land (7)
13. *Mack the _ _ _*, Bobby Darin song (5)
16. Prefix for a thousand (4)
18. Respectable (6)
20. Swoop (6)
22. Marvellous! (5)
23. Twin of Romulus (5)
25. Downpour (4)
27. Brick-holder (3)

Soldier On

AIDE
AIRMAN
BOMBER
CADET
COMMANDO
DRAGOON
ENGINEER
ENLISTED
FIGHTER
FOOT
GRENADIER
GUARDS-
MAN
GUERILLA
GUNNER
HERO
KNIGHT
MEN
MERCE-
NARY

OFFICER
PILOT
PRIVATE
RADIO
 OPERATOR
RANK AND FILE
RECRUIT
SCOUT

SIGNALMAN
SNIPER
TANKER
TROOPER
VETERAN
VOLUNTEER
WARMONGER
WARRIOR

```
E B R M E R C E N A R Y N D C
N N E A E L N A M S D R A U G
L N G K D O I R D G F T R E U
I W N I O I E F H E J U E T E
S A A G N C O R D T T O T A R
T R A R I E E O R N V C E V I
E R R F M N E O P O A S V I L
D I F E N O O R L E O K R R L
K O I U I P N U E D R E N P A
N R G K E D N G N B C A I A A
I E H R L T A A E R M L T I R
G P T E E E M N U R O O R O R
H I E E R M D I E T P M B Q R
T N R F O O T I Y R A V L A C
M S N C N A M L A N G I S T S
```

ACROSS

1. Secluded (6)
4. Climb (5)
7. Cutting tool (3)
8. Portion (7)
9. Put in order (7)
10. Escort (5)
13. Large book (4)
14. Leave (6)
16. Through (3)
17. Awkward (6)
20. Hoist (4)
23. Scoop (5)
25. Sanction (7)
26. A Flavouring (7)
27. Actor, _ _ _ Carmichael (3)
28. Pace (5)
29. Bomb-hole (6)

DOWN

1. Fight against (6)
2. TV character played by Tom Selleck (6)
3. Dentures (5)
4. Veer (6)
5. Order of business (6)
6. Suppose (6)
7. _ _ _ Wars, film (4)
11. Look to be (4)
12. Resentment (4)
14. Soggy (4)
15. Equestrian sport (4)
17. Swiss cottage (6)
18. Referee (6)
19. Impassive (6)
21. Install in office (6)
22. Kindling (6)
23. Actor, _ _ _ Penn (4)
24. Willow twig (5)

All Fall Down

ACORN
ACROBAT
APPLE
ARCHES
AVALANCHE
BONDS
CHIPS
CLOWN
COMET
CONE
CURTAIN
FLOP
HAIL
HAMMER
HOUSE
HUMPTY
  DUMPTY
JUMPER
LEAVES
LONDON
  BRIDGE
LOSER
METEOR
NEEDLE

NIGHT
NUT
PARACHUTE
PLAYER
POPULARITY
RAIN
RAMP
ROME
SLEET
SNOW

SOCKS
SPILL
STAR
STOCKS
STOCKINGS
SUN
TEMPERATURE
TIME
TUMBLE
WATERFALL

```
A C O R N P W A T E R F A L L
P C Q R L L R E P M U J L O E
P O R A P C C U R T A I N S A
L N Y O H A M M E R A D W E V
E E L E B O N D S H O Q O R E
R F S M M A C D P N W P L A S
U N L I J O T A B E O R C T G
T E E T M R R R H P N R H S N
A E E E O A I C U S S D I O I
R D T E C D N L T V T C P C K
E L T H G A A Q L H E O S K C
P E U E L R A M P I G S C S O
M T N A I R A I N R P I U K T
E U V T U M B L E N U S N O S
T A Y Y T P M U D Y T P M U H
```

ACROSS

1. Bicker (4,3)
4. Swamp (5)
7. Excercise period (4-3)
8. Cache (5)
9. Mummify (6)
12. Fragrant (8)
15. Actress in *Watching* (4,4)
17. Shriek (6)
18. *Two _ _ _ for Sister Sara*, film (5)
21. Tusked African pig (4,3)
22. Escapologist, _ _ _ Houdini (5)
23. Bit-by-bit (7)

DOWN

1. Character from *The Magic Roundabout* (8)
2. Back-scrubber (6)
3. Captured (4)
4. Nocturnal insect (4)
5. Author's payment (7)
6. Cargo's area (4)
10. Espouse (5)
11. Welsh county (5)
13. Felon (8)
14. Tinier (7)
16. Actor, _ _ _ Schwarzenegger (6)
18. Pulverise (4)
19. Oscillate (4)
20. Two-masted ship (4)

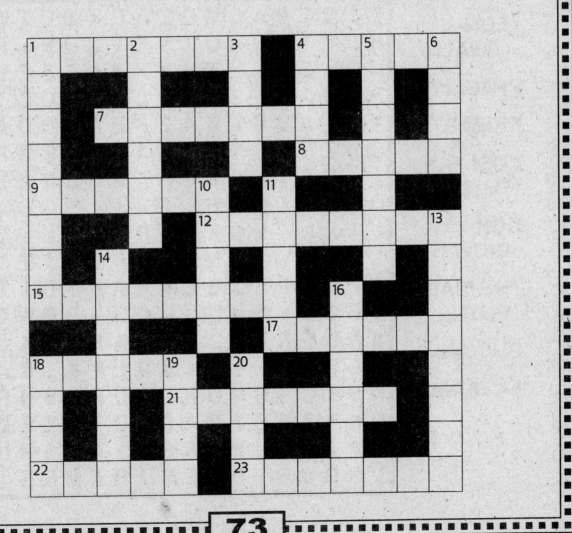

Composer Poser

Composers and their works are all to be found in this puzzle.

BIZET

CARMEN

THE PEARL FISHERS

DELIBES

COPPELIA

GOUNOD

FAUST

LEON-CAVALLO

I PAGLIACCI

MOZART

COSI FAN TUTTE

DON GIOVANNI

THE MAGIC FLUTE

PUCCINI

LA BOHEME

MADAM BUTTERFLY

TOSCA

ROSSINI

THE BARBER OF SEVILLE

WILLIAM TELL

VERDI

AIDA

LA TRAVIATA

OTELLO

RIGOLETTO

WAGNER

LOHENGRIN

THE RING

```
E I O I P A C M O Z A R T M C T W I
H L V T N O A O I T E Y O O H I R P
M O L E T I L T S V H N L E S E U H
R V B I D E S W A I L E P P O C I W
Y O I A V U L S A Z F E R M C D A I
S L Z N A E T O O M A A C I R G P L
I L F F I U S D G R W E N E N A L L
O E C R I R O F L I V I I T G G A I
L T H D E N G F O B R N E L U T M A
L O R P U T I N N R N F I O A T I M
A E M O R S T E E A E A N I D I T T
V O G D H V M U V H C B V D E W A E
A N B E N E N O B C O A R Y L A C L
C B R T H E I E I M R L P A I G A L
N S I O S G M O R T A U R W B N R S
O K B Z N S T R A P C D T O E E D V
E A I O E U F L A S H I A N S R H E
L G D D E T U L F C I G A M E H T T
```

ACROSS

1. Red Indian child (7)
7. Large wading bird (5)
8. Dumbfounded (7)
9. French brandy (6)
11. Filth (5)
13. Peal (4)
14. Capital of Kenya (7)
15. Printing recorrection (4)
16. Annoyed (5)
17. Painter (6)
21. Notifies (7)
22. Beach Boys song, _ _ _ John B (5)
23. Aerial (7)

DOWN

2. Electricity generator (10)
3. Salve (8)
4. Solicit (4)
5. Embargo (4)
6. Threadbare (4)
9. Villain (5)
10. Mariner (4,6)
12. Conflict (5)
13. Irritating (8)
18. Story (4)
19. Early (4)
20. Shortly (4)

Breakfast Time

ALL BRAN

ALPEN

BOWL

BREAKFAST

BROWN

CEREALS

CORN

CORNFLAKES

CRUNCHI-
NESS

EXERCISE

FLAVOUR

FRUIT

HONEY

KELLOGG'S

KILO

MAIZE

MILK

NICE

NUTS

RICE

SNACKS

SOGGY

SUGAR

TASTY

VALUE FOR
MONEY

VARIETY

VITAMINS

YOGHURT

```
V I T A M I N S S L A E R E C
A A S I W K I O M I L K I L O
L F R E D P C G C B L A T X R
U B C I G H E G I J B R O W N
E S R R E Q P Y O N R M L K F
F Z U E V T A S T Y A I W X L
O L I E A D Y C B A N Z C Y A
R A A A G K L S G G O L L E K
M I J V M W F E S I C R E X E
O A L M O W O A P Q R A G U S
N R S B T U V W S Y T X Y K Z
E A L P E N R D E T S I C B A
Y O G H U R T N F T G A U H I
X C O R N P O N U M N L K R J
C R U N C H I N E S S P E T F
```

ACROSS

1. Ornamental (10)
8. Large house (7)
9. Ventriloquist, _ _ _ DeCourcey (5)
10. Bovine animals (4)
11. Currency unit (4)
12. Perched (3)
14. Loving (6)
15. Eating apple (6)
18. Cut (3)
20. Lodgings (4)
21. US actress, _ _ _ Anderson (4)
23. Ethnic group (5)
24. Pierre _ _ _, former Canadian PM (7)
25. Smuggled goods (10)

DOWN

1. Dark cell (7)
2. US golfer, _ _ _ Beck (4)
3. Jean _ _ _, French film director (6)
4. Freshwater tortoise (8)
5. Las _ _ _, city in Nevada (5)
6. Endless life (11)
7. Conceited (11)
13. Tie (4,4)
16. Carry on (7)
17. Author, _ _ _ Christie (6)
19. Italian boxer, _ _ _ Carnera (5)
22. Chrysalis (4)

Dog Eared

ALSATIAN   GREAT DANE   PUG

BEAGLE   GREYHOUND   RETRIEVER

BORZOI   JACK RUSSELL   SALUKI

BOXER   LABRADOR   SCOTTIE

BULLDOG   LURCHER   SHEEPDOG

CHOW   MASTIFF   SPANIEL

COLLIE   PEKINGESE   TERRIER

CORGI   POINTER   WHIPPET

DACHSHUND   POODLE

```
B D A E I O F W P C D A I C A
U A D A C H S H U N D U E E L
L N C H O W A I G J B C D B S
L D E F L O L P U A I P S O A
D I S R L E U P S C V E G X T
O E F E I G K E H K G K R E I
G D E V E S I T E R R I E R A
T U L E B I V L E U E N Y L N
L O D I X Y T A P S A G H U E
O C O R G I T B D S T E O R L
S C O T T I E R O E D S U C G
B U P E F T Y A G L A E N H A
S B O R Z O I D Z L N N D E E
P O I N T E R O D O E N P R B
S P A N I E L R M A S T I F F
```

ACROSS

1. Ice-deposit (5)
7. Reveal (8)
8. Lacking originality (5)
10. Jousting match (10)
12. Crumple (8)
14. Pub drink (4)
16. Green gemstone (4)
17. Seven-sided polygon (8)
20. Exodus (10)
23. Flower part (5)
24. Money-saving (8)
25. Expressionless (5)

DOWN

1. Material (6)
2. Bench (4)
3. Wharf (4)
4. Scuffle (5)
5. Former gold coin (9)
6. Court fool (6)
9. Nearby (5)
11. Fighter in Roman arena (9)
13. Prosecute (3)
15. Crouch (5)
16. P.G. Wodehouse character (6)
18. Anthony _ _ _, British actor/singer (6)
19. Ancient Egyptian temple in Thebes (5)
21. Counterpart (4)
22. Eft (4)

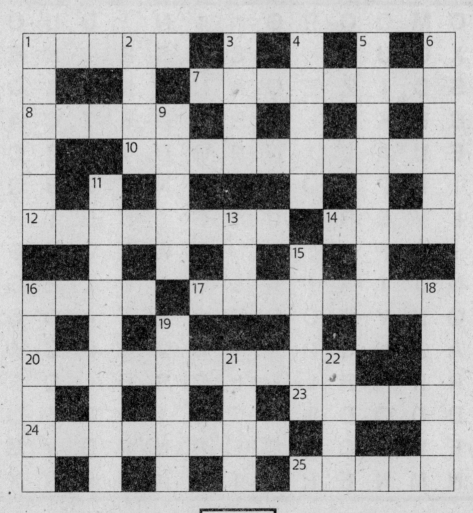

House Builder

BEAMS　　　　DOOR　　　　LOFT

BEDROOM　　　ELECTRIC　　　LOFT LADDER

BOILER　　　　FAN　　　　LOUNGE

CARPET　　　　FLOOR　　　　PLASTER

CEILING　　　　GARDEN　　　ROOF

CELLAR　　　　HEATING　　　SINK

CUPBOARDS　　HOUSE　　　　TILES

DINING ROOM　KITCHEN　　　WINDOWS

```
R O M O O R G N I N I D U O H
E X O U S R H C A S B I K E O
T S D I Z E O A U W P E A D U
S C E K V L T R F O B T C A S
A E U A L I N P W D I Y Z C E
L I P P L O M E I N V C B Q R
P L V E B B U T G I H E Y N E
B I S W N O L N F W L L H B D
E N J I A I A L G E U L E G D
D G H V F O O R C E T A O O A
R A A K Q O S T D M M R C W L
O R K R R L R L L O S D L O F T
O D D O D I M F O I U Z F O F
M E P I C E O F R N P O V B O
S N M N E H C T I K P S N X L
```

ACROSS

1. Partly cover something (7)
5. Duration (4)
9. Fruit much used in preserves (6)
10. Minimum (5)
12. Surpass (5)
13. Anchorage (7)
14. Convince (6)
16. Pertaining to race (6)
19. French castle (7)
21. Out-of-date (5)
23. Annoyed (5)
24. Paradoxical (6)
25. Container weight (4)
26. Italian red wine (7)

DOWN

2. Gymnastics discipline (5)
3. Ill-will (7)
4. Singer, _ _ _ Franklin (6)
6. Group of soldiers (7)
7. Suite composed by Tchaikovsky (10)
8. Stigma (4)
11. Royalist (10)
15. Good-for-nothing (7)
17. Milk pudding (7)
18. Travel show presenter, _ _ _ Chalmers (6)
20. Extremities (4)
22. A work period (5)

Notable

BARITONE   EUPHONIUM   SAXOPHONE

BASS CLEF   FLUTE   TREBLE CLEF

BRASS/BAND   HORN   TRIANGLE

CLARINET   MUSIC   TROMBONE

CORNET   PIANO   TRUMPET

CYMBALS   PICCOLO   TUBA

DRUMS   RECORDER   VIOLIN

```
T P Q Z P B R A S S T U B A S
R H E L I L S A X O P H O N E
E O N B A S S C L E F E X L C
B X O P N I N S F R O M H O Y
L N T R O M B O N E E L G E M
E J P I C C O L O K L M L V B
C C E N O T I R A B S G I R A
L N O P Q Z X R S T N O U E L
E V D R U M S V W A L X Y C S
F O V L N D C C I I V W P O W
H F L J O E K R N B A N D R N
B P O A I R T R U M P E T D N
E U P H O N I U M U V P R E R
V S T E N I R A L C Z Q S R O
S F L U T E S M U S I C O N H
```

ACROSS

3. Compliance (9)
8. Long-eared animal (4)
9. Blew up (8)
10. Summon back (6)
13. Brittle (5)
14. Livid (7)
15. Large sea-fish (3)
16. Instance (7)
17. Insignia (5)
21. Six-piece band (6)
22. Bus depot (8)
23. Musical tail-piece (4)
24. Formidable woman! (6-3)

DOWN

1. Temperament (9)
2. Down-to-earth (9)
4. Part of a wicket (5)
5. Swindle (7)
6. Peter _ _ _, *Ever Decreasing Circles* actor (4)
7. Music symbol (4)
11. Umbrella-shaped fungus (9)
12. Necessary (9)
14. Adversary (3)
15. Wash (7)
18. Colchester's county (5)
19. Hindu god (4)
20. Exclude (4)

Pot Black

BIG/BREAK
BLACK
BLUE
CUE
CUE BALL
CUE CASE
EXTENSION
FOUL
FOUR AWAY
GREEN

GREEN BAIZE
GREEN/CHALK
HALL
MATCH
MISS
ONE FOUR SEVEN
PINK
RED
REFEREE
SCREW

SIDE
SNOOKER
SPIDER
SWAN NECK
TIP
WHITE
WHITE GLOVES
YELLOW

```
N E E R G L K H D A W V B H E
O E N Y L P C C K L A H C I Y
W O V A N R A T E O T C I A G
H E H E A O L A D N U B W T R
I Z E H S L I M A E N A J N E
T I C D A R A S B F R A E X E
E A S E I T U A N U O E W Z R
G B C V U S L O O E R U I S E
L N R O A L E F F G T L U O F
O E E L W S B Y K E K X T A E
V E W N A W E A N N N N E P R
E R R C E L E T A B I O S U N
S G E E L R I R E D I P S P D
A U R O B S N O O K E R I T E
C G W K C A L B E U C T M O R
```

ACROSS

1. Contemplate (7)
4. P.D. _ _ _, crime writer (5)
7. Infer (7)
8. Lever open (5)
9. Protective plate (6)
12. Sufficient (8)
15. TV sitcom with Emma Wary and Paul Brown (8)
17. Composer of *The Messiah* (6)
18. Twenty per-cent (5)
21. Converted (7)
22. Hot, mixed drink (5)
23. Productive (7)

DOWN

1. Oriental carriage (8)
2. Actress, _ _ _ Bacall (6)
3. Hard work (4)
4. Military vehicle (4)
5. Enchanting (7)
6. Secure (4)
10. Film producer, _ _ _ Puttnam (5)
11. Lake in Northern Ireland (5)
13. Worker (8)
14. Crammed (7)
16. Discontent (6)
18. Baptismal basin (4)
19. Vague (4)
20. _ _ _ a Sixpence, film (4)

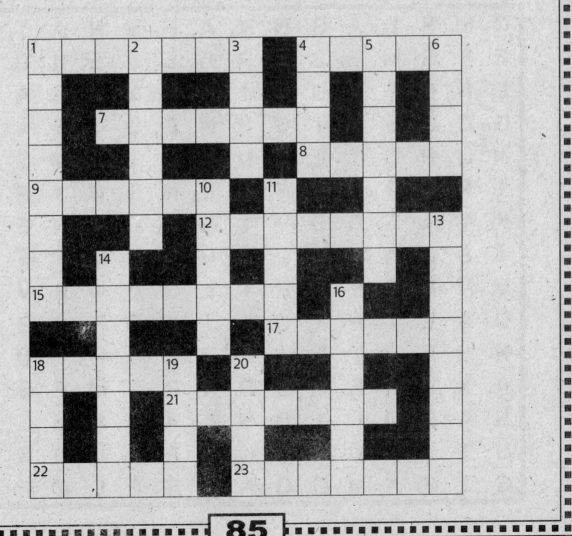

Space Programme

APOLLO
ASTEROID
ASTRONOMER
COMET
EARTH
FLASH
GEMINI
JUPITER
LEO
LIBRA

LIGHT
MARS
MERCURY
METEOR
MOON
NEPTUNE
ORION
PLUTO
SATURN
SCORPIO

SPACE
SPUTNIK
STARS
SUN
URANUS
VENUS
VIKING
VIRGO

```
O M F L A S H M A R S R A T N
E E S M E S O R L E L E N U S
L R C O V U T I S A N T G A R
G C O S A T U R N E O I E I A
N U R O T E H U O H I P M S T
I R P R O T Y S E N R U I R S
K Y I E R D V I R G O J N F E
I S O A N E P T U N E M I E A
V M E T E O R I L S U N E V S
U A L I L I G H T K G R C R T
R S P U T N I K R E O H T U E
A X U O E M O D K C T M E S R
N A B O L I B R A A U Q M E O
U T L F N L S K N P L U O K I
S I G A M O O N E S P D C E D
```

ACROSS

1. Strength (4)
4. Thrown (5)
7. At sea (6)
8. Chinese dog (4)
9. Yellowish gold (5)
10. Universal (6)
11. Dimensions (4)
12. Insulation material (5)
13. Vesta _ _ _, music hall star (6)
16. Stockade (4)
18. Actor, _ _ _ O'Neal (4)
19. Dilly-dally (6)
21. Sharp (5)
22. Explosive device (4)
24. Run scored in cricket (3-3)
25. Hag (5)
26. Central part (4)
27. Very sad (6)
28. Comedy actress, _ _ _ Blake (5)
29. Copied (4)

DOWN

1. Defending players (5)
2. US actress, Farrah _ _ _ (7)
3. Ordinary (6)
4. Thickset (6)
5. Despondent (7)
6. Small cucumber (7)
14. Meadow (3)
16. Film director, _ _ _ Ford Coppola (7)
17. Noisy (7)
18. _ _ _ of Sunnybrook Farm, novel (7)
19. Erase (6)
20. Tepee (6)
23. Mix together (5)

Battle Ground

The words in the following grid are associated with World War II.

ANVIL

ANZIO

ARNHEM

AXIS

BARBAROSSA

BISMARCK

BOUNCING BOMB

BULGE

CONVOY

CORAL/SEA

DESERT

RATS

DIEPPE

DUNKIRK

EL ALAMEIN

GOLD

IWO/JIMA

JUNO

KASSERINE

KURSK

MIDWAY

MONTE CASSINO

MONTY

OMAHA

OVERLORD

PATTON

ROMMEL

SEALION

SPITFIRE

SWORD

TOBRUK

TORCH

UTAH

```
O K O K W N I E M A L A L E D
L V S N U K R D A T N S G L R
T I E R U R A M I Z D L O K B
E A V R U J B S I E U G R A M
R F E N L K B O S B P I D O O
I Y L S A O A E T E K P N A B
F L E M M O R T A N R T E I G
T A M L D T B D U H E I S U N
I X O P R I A D H C A M N S I
P I N A O C R R A C A M M E C
S S T T W A O S N R O I O A N
U S Y T S M S R C H D N T L U
T H R O P I S K A W E L V I O
A R T N N J A H A L A M R O B
H C R O T N R Y L M O W I N Y
```

ACROSS

1. Courteous (6)
5. Chubby (3)
7. One who fails (5)
8. Furniture item (5)
9. Small freshwater fish (7)
13. Symbol for Leo (4)
14. Sizeable (5)
17. Encroach (6)
18. However (3)
19. Set afire (6)
20. Distress signal (5)
23. Receive (4)
25. Universal (7)
28. Brazen (5)
29. Proposals (5)
30. Striped insect (3)
31. David _ _ _, Tory politician (6)

DOWN

1. Reconnaissance unit (6)
2. Toil (6)
3. High voice (6)
4. Second-hand (4)
5. Vacant (4)
6. Hitchcock film, _ _ _ *Curtain* (4)
7. Trademark (4)
10. Module (4)
11. Judge's hammer (5)
12. Command (5)
15. Wrangle (5)
16. Fly without propulsion (5)
18. Second-class mark (4)
20. Frail (6)
21. Attack (6)
22. Any of two (6)
24. European mountains (4)
25. Snatch (4)
26. Part of the neck (4)
27. Genuine (4)

Gardening Tips

APPLE
ASTER
BARROW
BEANS
BLACKBERRIES
BLACKCURRANTS
BUCKET
CELERY
DAISY
LEEK

LILY
MOWER
ONIONS
PANSY
PARSNIPS
PEAR
PEAS
PLANTER
PLUM
RASPBERRIES

RHUBARB
ROLLER
ROSES
SOWING
SWEDE
TOMATOES
TULIPS
TURNIPS

```
R S P I N R U T Y E M P T Y E
O A A V E I P L A N T E R Z X
W E S T Z A I S Y S N A P E D
D A S P I L U T C O A S T E R
S A M A B E A N S W E D E W I
E U I R R E S A O I O S T U B
O C V S O K R R R N X R O A E
T P O N Y A K R U G I A R I U
A O J I E P E U I C W O S A L
M U L P L B U C K E T E N A B
O O R S K A E K H I S O P S A
T A W C B L U C K O B P L O N
O M A E E M Z A R O L L E R A
R L X R R U O L F E U I A E N
B A Y S R H U B A R B O T E A
```

ACROSS

6. Offer one's best wishes (12)
8. *Letter from _ _ _,* Proclaimers song (7)
9. Mixed drink (5)
10. Molten rock (4)
12. Signal fire (6)
14. Potholer (5)
15. Precious metal (6)
16. Staff of office (4)
19. Beginning (5)
21. Art of paper-folding (7)
22. Cooling cabinet (12)

DOWN

1. Short pause (8)
2. Wood pattern (5)
3. Drinking tube (5)
4. *The Glass _ _ _,* children's tale (7)
5. Dumbfound (4)
6. Popular dance of the twenties (10)
7. Suspended light (10)
11. Grate (3)
12. Beseech (3)
13. Indian thin flat loaf (8)
14. 100 runs in cricket (7)
17. Gatehouse (5)
18. Strand (5)
20. Toboggan (4)

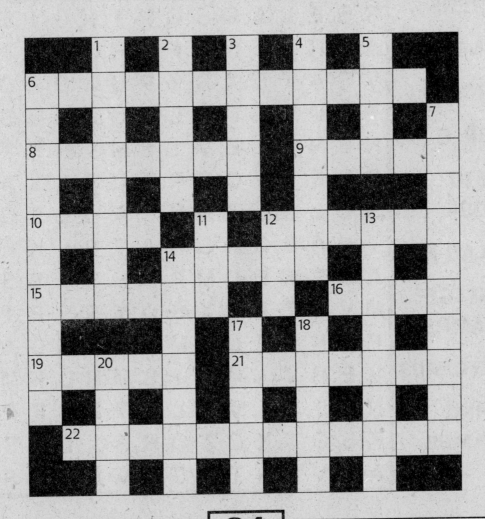

At the Post Office

ADVERTISEMENTS

BADGES

CALENDAR

CLOCK

DESK

EXPRESS POST

FORMS

LETTERS

MONEY

PARCELS

PEOPLE

PHOTO KIOSK

PILLAR BOX

POSTAGE STAMPS

POSTCARDS

SAVING STAMPS

SERVICE

STATIONERY

TELEPHONE BOX

TELEVISION

UNIFORM

VOUCHERS

WEIGHING SCALES

```
S S E L A C S G N I H G I E W
A T R E U N I F O R M X P P T
V S A T E X S T P U W O E O E
I R D T S D C L O C K B O S L
N E N E I E Y I S M T R P T E
G H E R V O E P T U S A L A P
S C L S L T N V C A O L E G H
T U A B G R O E A T P L K E O
A O C W E L M P R E S I S S N
M V S T A U X S D Y S P E T E
P A R C E L S M S S E G D A B
S E R V I C E I S M R O F M O
N O I S I V E L E T P J K P X
K S O I K O T O H P X L U S V
A D V E R T I S E M E N T S Y
```

ACROSS

1. On time (8)
5. Tenpin ball (4)
7. *Silver _ _ _*, David Soul hit (4)
8. Unknowing (8)
9. Middle (6)
12. Lean (7)
15. Muslim veil (7)
19. Gary _ _ _, golfer (6)
21. Milestone (8)
22. Excited (4)
23. Attire (4)
24. Dilapidated (8)

DOWN

1. Royal residence (6)
2. Burial vault (5)
3. Combine (5)
4. Capital city (6)
5. Interment (6)
6. Small (6)
10. Tidings (4)
11. Wander (4)
12. Printing fluid (3)
13. Spiral (4)
14. Children's game (1-3)
15. Colour (6)
16. Impede (6)
17. *Who's _ _ _ of Virginia Woolf?* film (6)
18. Panic (6)
19. Gambling game (5)
20. Make use of (5)

Fair Fun

AMUSEMENTS   FUN   RIDES

ARCADE   GYPSY CARAVAN   SHOWMEN

ARK   HORSE   SIDE SHOW

BALLOONS   HOT DOGS   TRACTION

BIG WHEEL   LIGHTS   ENGINE

CANDY   MUSIC   TWIST

CAROUSEL   PARATROOPER   WALTZER

DODGEMS   POPCORN

```
H N S E W C A N D Y W R E W B
O G O Y I N P S L Y A B A O N
T P G S H O W M E N L O M H A
D O U L I G H T S O T S U S B
O M F H B M E D U H Z P S E A
G P A R A T R O O P E R E D R
S L O B A S L D R F R A M I A
B Y H P R L C G A I B L E S C
I O N T C M T E C M D R N P Y
G S E W A O H M S L N E T O S
W D F I D S R S R F C A S P P
H O R S E T A N H K U W O S Y
E W A T W S C D C Y R N B V G
E N I G N E N O I T C A R T R
L T H I C S D S N O O L L A B
```

ACROSS

6. Now and then (12)
8. Forbearing (7)
9. Chomp (5)
10. Test (4)
12. Chess piece (6)
14. Indian tent (5)
15. _ _ _ *Impact*, Clint East film (6)
16. Sharp taste (4)
19. Poison (5)
21. Small flower (7)
22. Hard, sticky sweet (12)

DOWN

1. _ _ _ Yard, famous police HQ (8)
2. Valuable possession (5)
3. Inlet (5)
4. Shrub with fragrant flowers (7)
5. Open tart (4)
6. Airless (10)
7. Snapshot (10)
11. Actor _ _ _, Kingsley (3)
12. Beer cask (3)
13. Tip (8)
14. White ant (7)
17. Show mercy (5)
18. Sorceress (5)
20. Part of speech (4)

Well Preserved

BOTTLES

CHUTNEY

CONSERVE

FREEZE

FRUIT

HOME-MADE
  WINE

JAM

JARS

JELLY

KETCHUP

LABELS

MAR-
  MALADE

MINCEMEAT

NUTMEG

ONIONS

PECTIN

PEPPER

PICKLES

PRESERVES

RELISH

SALT

SAUCE

SPICES

SUGAR

SULTANAS

VEGETABLES

VINEGAR

```
V S C E N J P C P E C T I N V
N I O O E I H E E C U A S N E
U C N L N U S S P D N A R M G
T T L E T S E A A P S H A I E
M Y I N G L E O N W E R J N T
E R E U T A E R M A M R T D A
G Y E T R Z R I V A T L S S B
O R O S E F N P L E A L E A L
N B E E L C C A U S R L U S E
I H R L E E D Z E H K Z U S S
O F P M I E B C U C C G L E S
N J E C O S I A I H A T P R S
S A O R H P H P L R S E E R E
T M M E S E V R E S E R P K R
P U T E N I W E D A M E M O H
```

ACROSS
1. Elector (5)
5. Face shield (5)
8. Self-importance (3)
9., Prod (5)
10. *You Only Live _ _ _*, Bond novel (5)
11. Health resort (3)
12. Body organ (5)
15. Very small (6)
19. Apiece (4)
21. Tease (3)
22. Peel (4)
24. Tolerate (6)
28. Ruth _ _ _, *Hi-De-Hi!* actress (5)
31. Bark (3)
32. Marsh (5)
33. Scent (5)
34. Singer, _ _ _ Doonican (3)
35. Mephistopheles (5)
36. Written composition (5)

DOWN
1. Sufferer (6)
2. Golden red (6)
3. Feel remorse (6)
4. Part of a year (5)
5. Spirit drink (5)
6. Afternoon rest (6)
7. Capital of Saudi Arabia (6)
13. Brink (4)
14. Peruse (4)
16. Category (3)
17. Forearm bone (4)
18. Therefore (4)
20. Vehicle (3)
22. Needle (6)
23. Buy from abroad (6)
25. Snuggle (6)
26. Father of Saturn (6)
27. Use (6)
29. Engulf (5)
30. Bend (5)

Help Your Self

All of these items can go with the word "self".

ADDRESSED
APPOINTED
CONDUCT
CONFIDENCE
CONSCIOUS
CONTAINED
CONTROL
DENY
DISCIPLINE
DISCOVERY
DOUBT
DRIVEN
EDUCATED
EMPLOYED
ESTEEM
EVIDENT
GOVERN
HEAL
HELP
HYPNOSIS
IMAGE
IMPOSED
INDUCE
INTEREST

LESS
LOAD
LOVE
MADE
PITY
PLEASED
RESPECT
RESTRAINT

RISING
RULE
SAME
SERVICE
SERVING
START
TAUGHT
WILL

```
E E O C L G S U O I C S N O C
D M C C O N T A I N E D A O L
E A P V V N A D D R E S S E D
N S E L E D F W V E N G D C E
Y R E V O C S I D S F A A L T
N G R U R Y N L D P M A C M N
L E B E E G E L D E S O P M I
G T L D S Y L D L C N O M D O
E N N U T I E E C T D C E E P
C E I I R T S E R V I C E S P
U V P S A S C O N D U C T A A
D I S C I P L I N E L A S E P
N R U D N R V E H P R A E L N
I D I N T E R E S T Y L E P C
E V I D E N T T A U G H T H D
```

ACROSS

1. Redden (5)
4. Worship (5)
10. Molten rock (5)
11. Recreation time (7)
12. Demote (8)
13. French fashion designer (4)
15. Breakfast food (6)
17. Overlook (6)
19. Job (4)
20. Elegant (8)
23. A Shakespearian tragedy (7)
24. Unworldly (5)
25. Froth (5)
26. Irregularly-marked horse (5)

DOWN

2. Lawful (5)
3. Largest city in China (8)
5. Slow leak (4)
6. Stimulating (7)
7. Curse (11)
8. Shallow dish (5)
9. Sherlock Holme's hat (11)
14. Actor in *Shirley Valentine* (3,5)
16. Syrup given to babies (4-3)
18. Brush (5)
21. Makes advances (5)
22. Dark-purple (4)

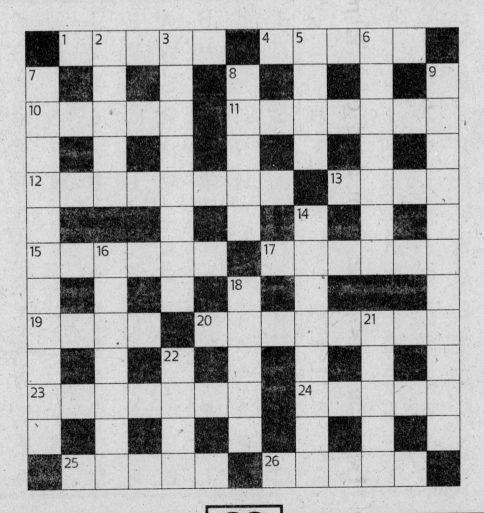

In the Office

CALCULATOR   FILING CABINET   RULER

CHAIR   LETTERS   STAMPS

COMPUTER   PAPER   STAPLER

DESKS   PENCILS   TELEPHONE

DISC   PENS   TIPPEX

ENVELOPE   PHOTOCOPIER   TYPEWRITER

FAX   PRINTER

```
F C O M P U T E R X C T T K F
S I T O Q A C U V W A Y E O A
P B L A R E L M D S L P L E X
E C A I P R S N K R C E E N M
N P R I N T E R D H U W P S O
C E L M B G A R A R L R H P T
I N K V S B C I X S A I O C I
L S T K L K R A T L T T N S P
S C S T A M P S B P O E E A P
R E R L I G U E G I R R P T E
D I S C B N D K B S N E L R X
I E L E T T E R S N R E C U S
K M E C D S T A P L E R T L D
E N V E L O P E K E A O P E S
P H O T O C O P I E R M O R O
```

Just a cryptic crossword

ACROSS

1. Accommodation providing help to repair a puncture (7,4)
9. The figure is unbroken (7)
10. Two-way revolver? (5)
11. Makes fun of bony parts (4)
12. Applied a rule for certain in an old drink (8)
14. Put off doctor without fee perhaps (5)
15. Sort of potato firm? (5)
20. Soft thing, to say the least (8)
22. She's the one with the broken arm (4)
24. Weapon British Rail put in a prepaid cover (5)
25. Payment for accommodation includes purpose to provide clothes (7)
26. Reprimanded for having been provided with site transport (5,2,4)

DOWN

2. Capable of being absorbed into the system? (7)
3. Six leave for the Spanish port (4)
4. Go wildly about one's business (6)
5. Extent of Terry's unusual woodwork (8)
6. Player found in a contractor's office (5)
7. Rows of drawers? (5)
8. Haughtiness found in a group of lions (5)
13. Barker's a capital chap! (8)
16. They arrange to work at the Post Office (7)
17. Movement caused when Dad's put in the Sergeant Major's company (5)
18. Cambridge college provides most of the wine (6)
19. Hates changing speed (5)
21. It's madder to chafe at a single article (5)
23. Conference suggesting limitation of food supplies (4)

Casualty

BEDS   FLOWERS   SICKNESS

BLOOD   HOSPITAL   STETHOSCOPES

BLOOD   MACHINES   TROLLEYS

PRESSURE   NURSE   VISITORS

CARDS   OPERATIONS   WARDS

CHARTS   PATIENTS   WHEELCHAIR

DOCTORS   PORTERS   X-RAY

```
S S E N K C I S A M Y B E D S
C S T E T H O S C O P E S T W
V O W K M A C H I N E S E W V
A I H N O R S E S S A R A I U
F B E S F T X N R A U R S S L
Y L E O N S O I R S D I O R A
A O L O P O U X S S R C X O T
R O C P R E A E E F S O E T I
X D H T E T R O L L E Y S I P
X U A S E P P A T I E N T S S
Q I I S D S R E T R O P O I O
N U R O M A T C H I P S H V H
N U O F L O W E R S O S E T E
N L C A R D S V S R D N O B R
B A M Y S R O T C O D X S H U
```

102

ACROSS

1. Legitimate (5)
4. Alarm (7)
8. Fish eggs (3)
9. Aristocratic (5)
10. Non-professional (7)
11. Scarce (6)
14. Lecturer (5)
16. Faulty (3)
18. Sickness (6)
19. Ragamuffin (6)
21. Chart (3)
22. Large dog (5)
25. Appear (6)
29. US comedy actress, _ _ _ Ball (7)
30. Hoarse (5)
31. Snow blade (3)
32. Violent storm (7)
33. Angler's basket (5)

DOWN

1. Deer meat (7)
2. The Scales [zodiac] (5)
3. Leftovers (5)
4. Fasten (4)
5. In pieces (5)
6. Provide medication (5)
7. Blunder (5)
12. Tree-gum (5)
13. Mild cheese (4)
15. Parent's brother (5)
17. Hoodwink (4)
20. Required (7)
22. Composer of *The Planets* suite (5)
23. Open sore (5)
24. Fourth Greek letter (5)
26. Sorcery (5)
27. Way (5)
28. Mexican currency (4)

My Son John

The words in the following grid are all the surnames of famous Johns.

ADAM

ALTMAN

BARRON

BETJEMAN

BIRD

BOWE

BUCHAN

BUNYAN

CLEESE

CONSTABLE

CRAVEN

CURRY

DONNE

DRYDEN

DUTTINE

FORTUNE

GIELGUD

GOODMAN

HURT

INMAN

JUNKIN

KEATS

KENNEDY

LENNON

MAJOR

MILTON

MORTIMER

PEEL

PILGER

STAPLETON

STONEHOUSE

THAW

TRAVOLTA

VINE

WAYNE

```
G R N T N P M L N D E E H D S
F O R E I A N A U O L N U P N
Y U O L D A M G J B T T N A J
H D G D M Y L E A O T L H O L
C E E T M E R T J I R C I E D
R N L N I A S D N T U B N M C
E A A G N N N E N B E N I U C
M B R Y O E N M I L O B R R I
I E A C N Y K C K N L R A N D
T N T R A U L W N R Y V M E M
R U S W R E B A U L E A N G A
O T T H E O L H J N N I L E D
M R A S W E N T R A V O L T A
D O E E E E S U O H E N O T S
S F K P K N O T E L P A T S H
```

ACROSS

1. Red pepper (8)
5. Motor-racing servicing area (4)
7. Small brook (4)
8. Enrol (8)
9. Encumber (6)
12. Army officer (7)
15. Spectre (7)
19. *Children of a _ _ _ God*, film (6)
21. Shrink (8)
22. Vaulting horse (4)
23. Period of time (4)
24. Subatomic particle (8)

DOWN

1. Cherry-red (6)
2. Sturdy (5)
3. John Le _ _ _, English author (5)
4. Rod Stewart hit, _ _ _ *May* (6)
5. Pulverising tool (6)
6. Light brown horse (6)
10. Irish songstress (4)
11. Abandoned (4)
12. Adhesive (3)
13. Unclothed (4)
14. Comedian, _ _ _ Abbot (4)
15. Courageous (6)
16. Flower secretion (6)
17. Heavily decorated (6)
18. Shattered (6)
19. Petrol unit (5)
20. Wooden-soled shoe (5)

Down...

All these words can go with DOWN.

AND OUT	HILL	TIME
BEAT	PAYMENT	TO EARTH
CAST	POUR	TO THE GROUND
FALL	RANGE	TOWN
FIELD	RIGHT	UNDER
GRADE	STAGE	WIND
HAUL	STAIRS	
HEARTED	THE LINE	

```
E A A N F N U U Q Y F U T K S
L I K H W S R I A T S U J T T
G P D O V H U L P H A I A O M
V W T D L E I F I L E G T T O
C Q I O R X Y L O T E H C U D
A N M T B H L F N R E N S O X
M M E H E J M E A G U L N D P
C H Y G A W M N R W E N A N F
V Z D I T Y G O G H N H D A Z
H W N R A E U F P D I L A E O
P V I P X N U A L H L T N U R
E O W B D K Q H J T E L S C L
X Z U P D E T R A E H E A A S
E D A R G Q R T R R T I X F C
U H H T R A E O T D F F V S S
```

106

ACROSS

1. Frisky (7)
5. Student (5)
8. 1950s actress, _ _ _ Bartok (3)
9. Amputate (5)
10. Memorise (5)
11. Poetry (5)
12. Type of race (5)
14. Abrupt (5)
15. Conspiracy (4)
17. Attire (5)
20. Expel (5)
22. Pen (4)
23. Utter (5)
24. Ventilated (5)
27. *The _ _ _ and the Dead*, novel (5)
29. Liquid measure (5)
30. Tycoon (5)
31. Knock (3)
32. Foe (5)
33 Completely (7)

DOWN

1. Conundrum (5)
2. Smithy's block (5)
3. Shuttle boat (5)
4. Added tax (4)
5. Paint-mixing board (7)
6. North American grasslands (7)
7. Merciful (7)
13. Go astray (3)
16. Human limb (3)
17. Disclose (7)
18. Letter from an Apostle (7)
19. Theatrical backdrop (7)
21. Sebastian _ _ _, runner (3)
24. Confess (5)
25. Kingly (5)
26. Dawdle (5)
28. Retained (4)

Enid Blyton

ADVENTURE   GEORGE   LUCY

ANNE   HOLS   MR. PLOD

AUNT/FANNY   JACK   MYSTERY

BIG EARS   JULIAN   NODDY

DICK   KIKI   PARROT

DOG   KIRRIN/ISLAND   SECRET/SEVEN

FAMOUS/FIVE   UNCLE QUENTIN

```
F I V E A B Z Y X J G E O O L
O A D V E N T U R E E G H U L
M N M Y S T E R Y D O G C B P
S B S O A A C S M P R Y L L U
R D E J U B P E R Q G U W O N
A F V Y Q S P C P M E X N Y C
E T E D X O O R L M J A C K L
G M N I E B C E O Y K M J N E
I N O C Q D F T D D I C K O Q
B O I K I R R I N D A Z C Y U
P A R R O T U W R O H S N B E
O E P X S I S L A N D N I T N
H O L S X M Y D N F A H U N T
I P R Q B M F G N F G T U U I
K I K I A Y C D E J U L I A N
```

ACROSS

1. Distinctly (7)
7. Bedtime drink (5)
8. Grazing area (7)
9. Cunning (6)
11. Abba member, _ _ _ Anderson (5)
13. In a frenzy (4)
14. Radioactive ore (7)
15. Friend (4)
16. Stingy (5)
17. Self-confidence (6)
21. Fulfil (7)
22. Pumpkin-like fruit (5)
23. Shaft (7)

DOWN

2. Guidance (10)
3. Supplement (8)
4. Fortune (4)
5. Crass person (4)
6. Pack animal? (4)
9. British actor, _ _ _ Blakely (5)
10. Considerate (10)
12. Sculptor, _ _ _ Epstein (5)
13. Aspiration (8)
18. E.C. Commissioner, _ _ _ Brittan (4)
19. Cricketer, _ _ _ Ramprakash (4)
20. Stringed instrument (4)

In the Swim

ARMBANDS FLOAT LIFE-JACKET

BACKSTROKE FREESTYLE LOCKERS

BREAST-STROKE GALA NOSE CLIP

BUTTERFLY GOGGLES SEA

CAP JUMP SWIMMING

COSTUME LESSONS SWIMMING POOL

DIVE LIFEBELT TOWEL

EVENT LIFEGUARD TRUNKS

```
S W I E L T E K C A J E F I L
E W E L Y T S E E R F M E L L
K B U T T E R F L Y L S A R E
O T L E B E F I L C O G R E K
R S E A L I F E G U A R D S O
T D I V M S K N U R T P S D R
S W I M M I N G P O O L N N T
K W D E I M F N G O W Y O A S
C S I N J E I E L A E N S B T
A R V M U L Y N N S L A S M S
B E E N M L S S E N E I E R A
E K V E P I P O O L Y N L A E
I C E S E L N O S E C L I P R
T O N S A L A G O G G L E S B
C L T Y E T T I E M U T S O C
```

ACROSS

6. Enterprising businessman (12)
8. Bauble (7)
9. Largest of the Greek islands (5)
10. Requirement (4)
12. Good cards to play? (6)
14. Exhausted (3,2)
15. Slovenly (6)
16. Ancient Peruvian (4)
19. Less dangerous (5)
21. Italian radio pioneer (7)
22. Political party (12)

DOWN

2. Grating, harsh (8)
2. Tropical lizard (5)
3. Packing case (5)
4. Mythical animal (7)
5. Govern (4)
6. Douse (10)
7. Cogent (10)
11. Laminated wood (3)
12. Actor, _ _ _ Healy (3)
13. Stringed instrument (8)
14. Oration (7)
17. Smug look (5)
18. Mutant (5)
20. _ _ _ Me To You, Beatles song (4)

Gone Fishing

ANGLER

BAG

BRANDLINGS

BREAD

COARSE

DRINKS

FISHERMAN

FLIES

FLOATS

GAFF

GROUND-
BAIT

HOLDALL

HOOKS

LANDING
NET

LUNCH

NYLON

REELS

REST

RODS

SALMON

SANDWICHES

SEAT

SPINNER

TROUT

UMBRELLA

WADERS

WEIGHTS

WELLINGTONS

```
A H O O P S E I L F Q N W W H
N A M R E H S I F U O E G O E
G V W I L O Z A I L L R L S J
L G B N L O G E Y L O D R S D
E N R O J K P N I U A A E U A
R I E M E S F N N L O H T N V
H O A L G D G D L C C R E S T
S P D A W T B Q K I O O A Q S
T A E S O A B R W U O V T E R
D I M N I S Z D T O D P N W E
R K S T L A N D I N G N E T D
I Y O E W A L L E R B M U X A
N C E K S Q B G S T H G I E W
K R E N N I P S K D A P U X I
S G N I L D N A R B H C N U L
```

ACROSS

1. Former name of *5 Across* (6)
5. Country bordering Iraq (4)
7. Sketched (5)
8. Large sea fish (4)
9. Hashish (4)
10. Value highly (5)
11. Viewpoint (6)
13. Impressionist, _ _ _ Bremner (4)
14. Stopped (6)
18. Ringed planet (6)
21. Stinging insect (4)
22. Floating aimlessly (6)
24. Sharpens (5)
25. Pudding (4)
26. Martial arts centre (4)
27. Selected (5)
28. Suffering (4)
29. Builds (6)

DOWN

1. Australian tennis star (3,4)
2. Digging tool (5)
3. Modify (5)
4. Provisions (7)
5. Acquire by bequest (7)
6. Fan (7)
12. Signal (3)
15. USA's 'Cotton' state (7)
16. Violent cyclonic storm (7)
17. Decorum (7)
19. Also (3)
20. Countries, states etc. (7)
22. Stage whisper (5)
23. Crest (5)

Sounds Right

Find the 46 animal sounds, including one hidden (not in the list) in the grid.

Hidden Word: C _____

Clue: A word for common conversation.

BELL
BELLOW
BLEAT
BLOW
BOOM
BRAY
BUZZ
CACKLE
CAW
CHEEP
CHIRP
CHIRRUP
CHUCK
CLUCK
COO
CROAK
CROW
DRONE
GABBLE
GAGGLE
GOBBLE
GRUNT
HISS
HONK

HOOT
HOWL
HUM
LOW
MEW
MOO
NEIGH

OINK
PURR
QUACK
ROAR
SCAPE
SCREAM
SNORT

SQUEAK
SQUEAL
TRUMPET
WHINNY
WHISTLE
YELP
YOWL

```
A K E P A C S N O R T C A R
B C R O A K U Q E L B B A G
B U Z Z R A O R U L W O Y W
C H A T T E R A M E G H O T
Y C M A E R C S E R A G H T
A L E C O K C A U Q R K A S
R L G R H G E N O R D N S G
B W O O N I T S U C H I R P
W O L W B E R P B H H O R Y
C H O E P B I R M E S T E N
I L O M H E L G U E L L T N
B M U H O L M E H P P L O I
I R A C N L A E U Q S R O H
T C A C K L E E L T S I H W
```

ACROSS

1. British statesman, _ _ _ Disraeli (8)
5. Camera's 'eye' (4)
7. Pulsate (5)
8. Run away (7)
9. Tease (9)
13. Ancient Mexican Indian people (4)
16. By way of (3)
17. Speck (3)
18. Hit song for the Village People (1.1.1.1)
21. Eight-sided (9)
24. Ministerial assembly (7)
26. Compose (5)
27. Tale (4)
28. Courageous (8)

DOWN

1. Ian _ _ _, cricketer (6)
2. Location of Oslo (6)
3. Monastic head (5)
4. Capture (3)
5. Neighbourhood (8)
6. Marsh grass (5)
8. Fitting (3)
10. US state, capital Boise (5)
11. Asian country (5)
12. Dusting powder (4)
14. Actor, _ _ _ Guinness (4)
15. Flying (8)
19. Seafaring (6)
20. Estimate (6)
21. Baroness _ _ _, author of The Scarlet Pimpernel (5)
22. Kernel (3)
23. Further down (5)
25. Sprite (3)

Train of Thought

BRANCH

COAL

DRIVER

ENGINE

FARE

FREIGHT

GRADIENT

GREAT
    WESTERN

HISS

HISTORY

JOURNEY

JUNCTION

LINE

LOAD

MAIN

NETWORK

PASSEN-
    GERS

PLATFORM

PULL

RAILWAY

RIDE

ROAR

ROUTE

SIGNAL

SMELL

SMOKE

STATION

STEAM TRAIN

TICKET

TRACK

TRAVEL

TRIP

TUNNEL

VAN

WAGON

WHISTLE

```
A S T N E I D A R G K C A R T
D R I V E R Y M R O F T A L P
W S C L E V A R T J A L N S L
N R K K R S W E T U O R I T A
R E E H M L L U P I E L A A N
E G T O G L I T A M L E R T G
T N K V E R A F N U T N T I I
S E N M N B R N O Y S N M O S
E S S O I D H T E P I U A N Y
W S P W G C A N H T H T E N R
T A L V N A R O R G W L T I O
A P A A E U W C L I I O S A T
E N R D O P I R T N D E R M S
R B Y J E C X F E Q Z E R K I
G S S I H N O I T C N U J F H
```

ACROSS

1. Riotous (10)
8. Large meal (7)
9. Endangered animal (5)
10. Water jug (4)
11. Chimer (4)
12. Hatchet (3)
14. Discernible (6)
15. _ _ _ Weapon, Mel Gibson film (6)
18. Container (3)
20. Nimble-fingered (4)
21. Plug (4)
23. Coarse (5)
24. Worry (7)
25. Gas mask (10)

DOWN

1. Paul _ _ _, TV magician (7)
2. Garden pest (4)
3. Scoundrel (6)
4. Trellised trees (8)
5. Singer, _ _ _ Ronstadt (5)
6. Building for celestial studies (11)
7. Heavy with moisture (11)
13. Adversity, suffering (8)
16. Transporter (7)
17. Illicit romance (6)
19. Entertainer, _ _ _ Forsyth (5)
22. Fleece (4)

Watch with Mother

Find the 33 children's TV programmes.

ANDY PANDY

BATMAN

BLACK/BEAUTY

BLUE PETER

CRACKERJACK

DR. WHO

FLIPPER

FLOWERPOT MEN

GRANGE/
 HILL

JACKANORY

LASSIE

LONE
 RANGER

MAGPIE

MUFFIN
 THE MULE

MUPPETS

ORLANDO

PICTURE/
 BOOK

PINKY AND
 PERKY

POGLES
 WOOD

POSTMAN
 PAT

RAG, TAG
 AND/BOBTAIL

RAINBOW

ROBIN HOOD

SESAME/STREET

SOOTY

THE
 FLINTSTONES

THUNDERBIRDS

TOM AND
 JERRY

TOP CAT

WOMBLES

WONDER/
 WOMAN

WOODENTOPS

YOGI BEAR

```
S L A S S I E R T A P N A M T S O P
L S P O T N E D O O W K A B L L I H
M I D N A G A T G A R G C Y E N A K
N F A L A S D L U R P F D A K P C B
O A L T O M E Z B I A N L Y L A E Y
S T M O B S O L E W A N A I J B L M
T Y T T W O U W B P O N G R P C U A
H Y R O A E B Q Y M D N E E Y P M Y
U K O O P B R D V P O K D O P W E R
N D W E N A N P E M C W G E H O H R
D K T F J A I R O A Y I T A R B T E
E E O E N C K R R T B S P X I N N J
R T H O T Y L C U E M A S E S I I D
B G W U B A I A A T E E R T S A F N
I D R Y N L E R O J A H N E C R F A
R E D D F B R E G N A R E N O L U M
D O O H N I B O R D T A C P O T M O
S E N O T S T N I L F E H T G K I T
```

ACROSS

1. Manufactured article (7)
5. Flog (4)
9. Subordinate (6)
10. *& 8 Down* England batsman (5,4)
12. Rope-tie (5)
13. Book repository (7)
14. Run out (6)
16. Open shoe (6)
19. Instalment (7)
21. Municipal (5)
23. Subside (5)
24. Water-gate (6)
25. Watched (4)
26. *Man of _ _ _,* Shadows hit (7)

DOWN

2. Cheek colouring (5)
3. *High Plains _ _ _,* Clint Eastwood film (7)
4. Ring (6)
6. European country (7)
7. First postage stamp (5,5)
8. *See 10 Across*
11. Quicken (10)
15. Confidential (7)
17. Version (7)
18. *Ferry Across the _ _ _,* song (6)
20. Portent (4)
22. Churchman (5)

Scrabble

BLANK	PLAYERS	SQUARES
BOARD	POINTS	TILES
DICTIONARY	RACKS	TRIPLE
DOUBLE	RULES	TURN
GAME	SCORE	VALUES
LETTERS	SCRABBLE	WINNER
OPPONENTS	SKILL	WORDS

```
B C T O Q P A E C D B O A R D
Z B U C P L A Y E R S P Q E I
S E R A U Q S A C R D E I H C
H E N I S W X E E L L P O A T
A M L E L B T T J P M O N P I
V A L U E S T N I O P E Q T O
V G Z A X E O R L L N N P Q N
E T S F L V T Y E R E A E T A
L A K G L W M W D O E S M O R
B E C I I E G O W P C N A N Y
B L A N K S H P I O B A N E S
A Z R A S Q F A R I R E S I T
R I D O U B L E J E C D I Q W
C Q T U E H E D R U L E S T A
S T N E N O P P O Z D Q A E O
```

ACROSS
1. Historical records store (8)
5. Typical pattern (4)
7. Saintly ring (4)
8. Space (8)
9. Emblem (6)
12. Emptiness (7)
15. Intricate or complicated (7)
19. Act correctly (6)
21. The study of religion (8)
22. Nil (4)
23. Whetstone (4)
24. Michael Jackson album (8)

DOWN
1. Thunder-struck (6)
2. Nuclear weapon (1-4)
3. Spoken (5)
4. Actress, _ _ _ Loren (6)
5. Actress, _ _ _ Pagett (6)
6. Distress signal (6)
10. Mutilate (4)
11. Egg-shaped (4)
12. Annoy (3)
13. Lane-marker (4)
14. American space agency (4)
15. Walking aid (6)
16. Conditional release from prison (6)
17. Exertion (6)
18. Diversion (6)
19. Purchaser (5)
20. Type of nut (5)

ABC Girls

ANGELA JOYCE STELLA
BEATRICE KATE TRACY
CAROL LILY URSULA
DIANE MARY VERA
EMMA NORMA WINIFRED
FREDA OLIVE XANIA
GERTRUDE PHYLLIS YOLANDE
HELEN QUEENIE ZETA
IRENE RUTH

```
A L L E T S M B E A T R I C E
E N A I D C P L E Z X F O A C
A P G R L M N B A H U T P R Y
R A B E R O L I V E Q N P O O
E S I N L M L E F L D B Z L J
V K V E M A R Y L E O A O E Z
D E R F I N I W L N M P D Q R
Q U E E N I E F A R F N R S U
K A T E A B R L O D A L I P T
P S T E F E U N X L Z L Q R H
Z R M O D S O Q O J L G A L P
E M M A R C O Y S Y O C R C J
T J R U T L S K H K Y M O K B
A P L I L Y T P R L U X P G F
G E R T R U D E R P X A N I A
```

ACROSS

1. Long-eared animal (6)
4. Wreckage (6)
7. Spiritual teacher (4)
8. Abound (4)
10. *A Night at the _ _ _,* film (5)
11. Peter _ _ _, goalkeeper (7)
14. Soft cap (3)
15. Rescued (5)
17. Pigtail (5)
18. Greek woodland god (5)
19. Tree (3)
21. Ruler (7)
24. Fringe-benefits (5)
26. Wound mark (4)
28. Level (4)
29. Ordinary seaman (6)
30. Peril (6)

DOWN

1. Temporary ruler (6)
2. Sweep (5)
3. Full amount (5)
4. Perish (3)
5. The Eternal City (4)
6. Maroon (6)
9. Ogre (7)
11. Smudge (4)
12. Sway, influence (7)
13. Vagabond (5)
16. Swerve (4)
18. Late meal (6)
20. Style (6)
22. Went astray (5)
23. Mass of water (5)
25. Corrosion (4)
27. Gear tooth (3)

Winter Wear

ANORAK

BALACLAVA

BERET

CAP

CAPE

CARDIGAN

CLOAK

COAT

COSY

DRY

FAKE-FUR

GLOVES

HAT

HOOD

JUMPER

LONG-
JOHNS

MAC

MITTENS

MUFFLER

SCARF

SKI-SUIT

SNOOD

SNOW-SHOES

SNUG

SOCKS

SWEATER

VEST

WARM

WATERPROOFS

WELLINGTONS

```
A A Q S F O O R P R E T A W S
V E P A C Q Z W C S X S G E K
A D C C L P R O V F N N L D I
L T A N O R A K T E D O O N S
C G R B A T Y C T H N T V U U
A M D E K J M T L J M G E B I
L U I H P R I I O K O N S E T
A F G L A M P R N Q A I R R Z
B F A W S T U Q G C D L E E W
Y L N V S F D J J O H L T T S
F E Z H E Y C M O S Y E A B D
H R W K O S A H H Y N W E G X
N M A X O C T D N K P L W T D
J F L C S E O H S W O N S R R
S O C K S R G U N S T T Y V F
```

ACROSS

1. Toe-rags! [anag] (7)
7. Petrol unit (5)
8. Bartered (7)
9. Minuscule (6)
11. Paroxysm (5)
13. Tread (4)
14. Previous (7)
15. Fibber (4)
16. Country bordering Turkey (5)
17. Higher-ranking (6)
21. Song and dance show (7)
22. Comedian, _ _ _ Hill (5)
23. Recorders of *Night Fever* (3,4)

DOWN

2. Acrobatics apparatus (10)
3. Names book (8)
4. Neutral tint (4)
5. Singer, _ _ _ Te Kanawa (4)
6. Hindustani (4)
9. Two crotchets (5)
10. Threefold (10)
12. Richard _ _ _, *Stir Crazy* actor (5)
13. Freshwater food fish (8)
18. Lowest tide (4)
19. Boat propellers? (4)
20. Entice (4)

SOLUTIONS

PUZZLE 1

Across: 1, Despised, 5. Viva, 7. Dell, 8. Limerick, 9. Comedy, 12. Jealous, 15. Gherkin, 19. Bernie, 21. Debonair, 22. Gulp, 23. Same, 24. Traverse.

Down: 1. Deduct, 2. Pulse, 3. Sally, 4. Dimple, 5. Verbal, 6. Ankles, 10. Mire, 11. Dark, 12. Jan, 13. Anne, 14. Oven, 15. Guides, 16. Remove, 17. Impact, 18. People, 19. Burma, 20. Rogue.

PUZZLE 5

Across: 1. Flare, 4. Chops, 10. Powys, 11. Harness, 12. Ceremony, 13. Capo, 15. Affirm, 17. Gandhi, 19. Uses, 20. Pavement, 23. Assuage, 24. Davro, 25. Tawny, 26. Crush.

Down: 2. Lower, 3. Rosemary, 5. Hard, 6. Piebald, 7. Spectacular, 8. Rhine, 9. Association, 14. Calendar, 16. Freesia, 18. Caged, 21. Elvis, 22. Pain.

PUZZLE 9

Across: 1. Indiscreet, 8. Saviour, 9. Morse, 10. Arid, 11. Room, 12. Sap, 14. Sleeve, 15. Beacon, 18. Net, 20. Real, 21. Mini, 23. Title, 24. Scalpel, 25. Microscope.

Down: 1. Invoice, 2. Door, 3. Sermon, 4. Remember, 5. Earns, 6. Assassinate, 7. Responsible, 13. Overhear, 16. Cripple, 17. Kansas, 19. Tutti, 22. Halo.

PUZZLE 2

PUZZLE 6

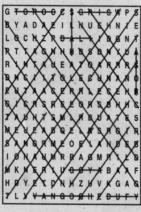

PUZZLE 10

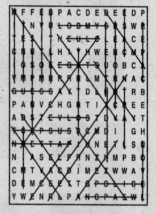

PUZZLE 3

Across: 1. Samba, 7. Baritone, 8. Aglow, 10. Tournament, 12. Smallpox, 14. Near, 16. Dock, 17. Cardigan, 20 . Stupendous, 23. Roost, 24. Gargoyle, 25. Serve.

Down: 1. Status, 2. Boot, 3. Pair, 4. Midas, 5. Sovereign, 6. Fetter, 9. World, 11. Sanctuary, 13. Ova, 15.Odour, 16. Design, 18. Nettle, 19. Venom, 21. Dull, 22. Sore.

PUZZLE 7

Across: 3. Elton John, 8. Sent, 9. Dwelling, 10. Rouble, 13. Churn, 14. Snowdon, 15. Dog, 16. Shallow, 17. Lucre, 21. Cartel, 22. Dinosaur, 23. Food, 24. Unsettled.

Down: 1. Ostracise, 2. Inaugural, 4. Laden, 5. Opening, 6. Jolt, 7. Hunt, 11. Education, 12. Interlude, 14. Sow, 15. Dormant, 18. Scree, 19. Sign, 20. Pose.

PUZZLE 11

Across: 1. Gushed, 7. Apiarist, 8. Toucan, 9. Grip, 10. Lace, 12. Clay, 14. Tall, 16. Roger, 18. Viola, 21. Star, 24. Cope, 26. Moth, 27. Visa, 28. Zenith, 29. Commando, 30. Naples.

Down: 1. Got out, 2. Squall, 3. Danger, 4. Rising, 5. Vital, 6. Study, 11. Alive, 12. Crest, 13. Alda, 15. Alto, 17. Oil, 19. Orient, 20. Amazon, 22. Thrill, 23. Riches, 24. Crack, 25. Prime.

PUZZLE 4

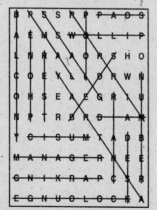

PUZZLE 8

PUZZLE 12

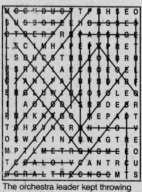

The orchestra leader kept throwing tempo tantrums.

126

SOLUTIONS

PUZZLE 13

Across: 1. Aston, 4. Wrath, 10. Eyrie, 11. Avarice, 12. Sapphire, 13. Cost, 15. Nimbus, 17. Belief, 19. Link, 20. Cosmetic, 23. Terrain, 24. Upset, 25. Whelk, 26. Chant.

Down: 2. Strap, 3. Overhaul, 5. Real, 6. Tripoli, 7. Personality, 8. Zaire, 9. Certificate, 14. Vermouth, 16. Monarch, 18. Bound, 21. Tyson, 22. Ball.

PUZZLE 17

Across: 1. Yorkshire, 6. Boa, 8. Costa, 9. Choir, 10. Peter, 11. Pest, 13. Verse, 15. Rifle, 17. Vital, 19. Delve, 21. Myth, 23. Nasty, 26. Stole, 27. Brute, 28. Elf, 29. Propeller.

Down: 1. Yacht, 2. Reserved, 3. Shaver, 4. Inch, 5. Elope, 6. Bumper, 7. Brat, 12. Sea, 14. Eventual, 16. Ivy, 18. Lay off, 20. Liable, 21. Mast, 22. Troop, 24. Sneer, 25. Nero.

PUZZLE 21

cross: 1. Harassed, 5. Mess, 8. East, 9. Terrapin, 10. Address, 13. Drake, 14. Local issues, 18. Rifle, 19. Reduced, 23. Annalist, 24. Long, 25. Eyes, 26. Empanels.

Down: 1. Hyenas, 2. Rased, 3. Sales, 4. Dart, 6. Expiate, 7. Sunset, 11. Erase, 12. Skier, 13. Dosed, 15. Offence, 16. Crease, 17. Adages, 20. Estop, 21. Clove, 22. Kite.

PUZZLE 14

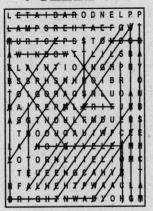

PUZZLE 18

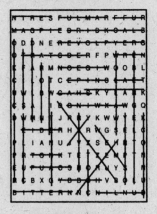

PUZZLE 22

PUZZLE 15

Across: 1. Poached, 4. Covet, 7. Treacle, 8. Wheat, 9. Peseta, 12. Portrait, 15. Enormous, 17. Hurdle, 18. Lapel, 21. America, 22. Fussy, 23. Diverse.

Down: 1. Postpone, 2. Carpet, 3. Dick, 4. Chew, 5. Veteran, 6. Tent, 10. Apron, 11. Fresh, 13. Tiresome, 14. Compass, 16. Creche, 18. Loaf, 19. Lady, 20. Lend.

PUZZLE 19

Across: 1. Prepare, 5. Door, 9. Sweets, 10. Among, 12. Dense, 13. Utensil, 14. Impede, 16. Simmer, 19. Initial, 21. Habit, 23. Total, 24. Cubism, 25. Rare, 26. Editing.

Down: 2. Rowan, 3. Pretend, 4. Rescue, 6. Opossum, 7. Regularity, 8. Pace, 11. Administer, 15. Pointer, 17. Inhabit, 18. Sliced, 20. Isle, 22. Basin.

PUZZLE 23

Across: 1. Jurassic, 5. Goad, 7. Cool, 8. Onlooker, 9. Battle, 12. Memphis, 15. Piebald, 19. Cement, 21. Occupied, 22. Rasp, 23. Tina, 24. Sprinkle.

Down: 1. Jacobi, 2. Allot, 3. Smoke, 4. Collie, 5. Grow up, 6. Dermis, 10. Tide, 11. Lima, 12. Mud, 13. Mole, 14. Hire, 15. Pay out, 16. Beluga, 17. Lyrics, 18. Staple, 19. Cider, 20. Moron.

PUZZLE 16

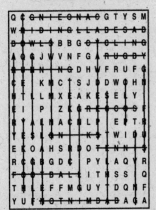

PUZZLE 20

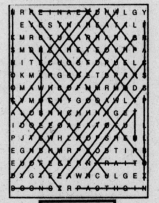

PUZZLE 24

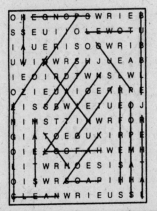

SOLUTIONS

PUZZLE 25

Across: 1. Failing, 4. Baird, 7. Uncouth, 8. Tyler, 9. Slalom, 12. Evacuate, 15. Diagnose, 17. Scathe, 18. Build, 21. Allergy, 22. Misty, 23. Spaniel.

Down: 1. Famished, 2. Lonely, 3. Glum, 4. Boht, 5. Italian, 6. Dour, 10. Melon, 11. Bates, 13. External, 14. Various, 16. Jargon, 18. Boom, 19. Davy, 20. Alas.

PUZZLE 29

Across: 3. Scrapbook, 8. Pelt, 9. Unstable, 10. Reason, 13. Morse, 14. Blemish, 15. Cot, 16. Nosegay, 17. Cream, 21. Canada, 22. Saturate, 23. Clan, 24. Personnel.

Down: 1. Apartment, 2. Albatross, 4. Count, 5. Assault, 6. Brag, 7. Oils, 11. Miserable, 12. Champagne, 14. Boy, 15. Captain, 18. Scene, 19. Pale, 20. Fuss.

PUZZLE 33

Across: 1. Visible, 5. Slam, 7. Bite, 8. Cairn, 9. Neil, 10. Duel, 12. Defence, 14. Turkey, 18. Ole, 19. Eleven, 23. Student, 25. Gold, 26. Taxi, 27. Genoa, 28. Nile, 29. Drag, 30. Margate.

Down: 1. Vacant, 2. Sailor, 3. Bundle, 4. Ebbed, 5. Sentence, 6. Melee, 11. Levee, 13. Care, 15. Unit, 16. Kindling, 17. Young, 20. Leger, 21. Vienna, 22. Negate, 23. Sated, 24. Totem.

PUZZLE 26

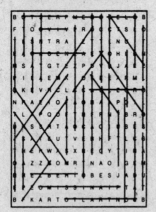

PUZZLE 30

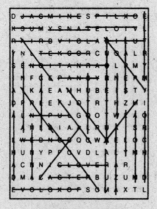

PUZZLE 34

PUZZLE 27

Across: 1. Strong, 5. Mame, 7. Ratio, 8. Reel, 9. None, 10. Norma, 11. Needed, 13. Riga, 14. Embark, 18. T-shirt, 21. Asia, 22. Clever, 24. Pulse, 25. Plot, 26. Gigi, 27. Ernie, 28. Feed, 29. Stroke.

Down: 1. Syringe, 2. Oiled, 3. Grind, 4. Attract, 5. Monarch, 6. Manager, 12. Err, 15. Moselle, 16. Adapted, 17. Killing, 19. Sol, 20. Turbine, 22. Cedes, 23. Elgar.

PUZZLE 31

Across: 1. Bob Hope, 5. Cower, 8. Acted, 9. Brian, 10. Model, 11. Hinge, 13. Extol, 14. Nose, 17. Peseta, 19. Recent, 22. Fern, 24. Omaha, 26. Cubed, 29. Growl, 30. Henna, 31. Orson, 32. Three, 33. Dresser.

Down: 1. Beach, 2. Baton, 3. Oddment, 4. Exodus, 5. Cable, 6. Whistle, 7. Ringlet, 12. Ire, 15. Oaf, 16. Err, 17. Prophet, 18. Spanner, 20. Enclose, 21. Nee, 23. Eroded, 25. Agave, 27. Basis, 28. Donor.

PUZZLE 35

Across: 3. Hampshire, 8. Room, 9. Specimen, 10. Dakota, 13. Avoid, 14. Forsake, 15. Bat, 16. Lucifer, 17. Alice, 21. Regina, 22. Detonate, 23. Much, 24. Degrading.

Down: 1. Gradually, 2. Cockroach, 4. Assay, 5. Pierrot, 6. Heir, 7. Reek, 11. Malicous, 12. Telepathy, 14. Far, 15. Bernard, 18. Green, 19. Mere, 20. Poor.

PUZZLE 28

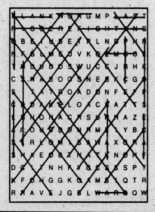

PUZZLE 32

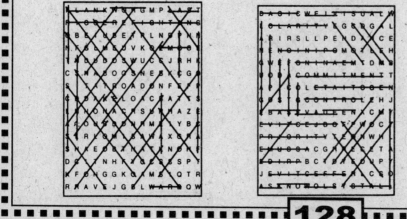

PUZZLE 36

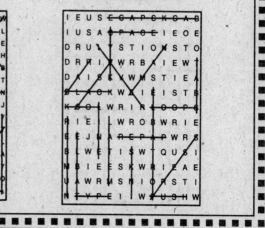

SOLUTIONS

PUZZLE 37

Across: 1. Goalkeeper, 8. Egotism, 9. Nadir, 10. Slum, 11. Knit, 12. Web, 14. Uneasy, 15. Dispel, 18. Alf, 20. Atom, 21. Fist, 23. Cling, 24. Lumbago, 25. Fraternity.

Down: 1. Globule, 2. Axis, 3. Kimono, 4. Einstein, 5. Endow, 6. Reassurance, 7. Tribulation, 13. Escargot, 16. Privacy, 17. Popular, 19. Flier, 22. Impi.

PUZZLE 41

Across: 1. Molasses, 5. Fair, 7. Done, 8. Animated, 9. Sultry, 12. Jehovah, 15. Battery, 19. Bolero, 21. Distaste, 22. Pits, 23. Roan, 24. Atkinson.

Down: 1. Medusa, 2. Agent, 3. Scary, 4. Stifle, 5. Franco, 6. Radish, 10. Loot, 11. Rife, 12. Jay, 13. Hobo, 14. Vile, 15. Border, 16. Triton, 17. Russia, 18. Robson, 19. Break, 20. Lupin.

PUZZLE 45

Across: 1. Dogged, 5. Hops, 7. Reeve, 8. Rope, 9. Ante, 10. Alert, 11. Ascend, 13. Heel, 14. Tomato, 18. Parang, 21. Fear, 22. Parade, 24. Eliza, 25. Gala, 26. Dell, 27. Glenn, 28. Flue, 29. Turban .

Down: 1. Dormant, 2. Geese, 3. Dread, 4. Develop, 5. Heather, 6. Pattern, 12. Net, 15. Overall, 16. Acreage, 17. Officer, 19. Aga, 20. Gremlin, 22. Paint, 23. Rider.

PUZZLE 38

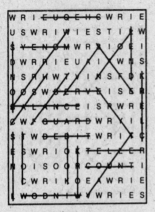

PUZZLE 42

Cumbrian Lake: Derwent Water.

PUZZLE 46

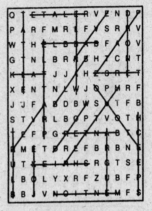

PUZZLE 39

Across: 1. Protect, 5. Feed, 9. Europe, 10. Augur, 12. Theft, 13. Calling, 14. Outcry, 16. Red-hot, 19. Granted, 21. Toper, 23. Own up, 24. Agreed, 25. Drew, 26. Idolise.

Down: 2. Rouse, 3. Trotter, 4. Clench, 6. English, 7. Derogatory, 8. Bail, 11. Stronghold, 15. Trainee, 17. Enthral, 18. Edward, 20. Type, 22. Press.

PUZZLE 43

Across: 1. Smite, 4. Tweak, 10. Tired, 11. Imperil, 12. Molineux, 13. Join, 15. Lavish, 17. Tom-tom, 19. Term, 20. Unlawful, 23. Neighed, 24. Dixie, 25. Dolph, 26. Bride.

Down: 2. Moral, 3. Tidiness, 5. Wept, 6. Airport, 7. Stimulating, 8. Minus, 9. Glenn Miller, 14. Pomander, 16. Vertigo, 18. Anode, 21. Fixed, 22. Chop.

PUZZLE 47

Across: 1. Whisper, 5. Crow, 9. Prompt, 10. Aspen, 12. Shell, 13. Respite, 14. Impure, 16. Damage, 19. Anaemia, 21. Plant, 23. Irons, 24. Shanty, 25. Niki, 26. Predict.

Down: 2. Horse, 3. Similar, 4. Entire, 6. Replica, 7. Winceyette, 8. Mars, 11. Estimation, 15. Peacock, 17. Applaud, 18. Caesar, 20. Mask, 22. Attic.

PUZZLE 40

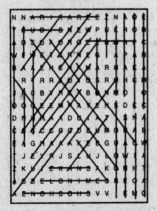

PUZZLE 44

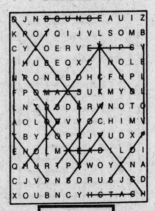

PUZZLE 48

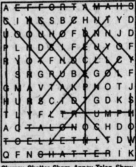

Clumsy, Chatter, Sham, Annoy, Talon, Show, Effort, Contradict, Control, Deception, Upright, Intellect, Cost, Likely, Student, Chide, Hush, Dull, Honorary, Triumph.

SOLUTIONS

PUZZLE 49

Across: 6, Aristocratic, 8. Amalgam, 9. Madge, 10. Erin, 12. Flimsy, 14. Peril, 15. Rental, 16. Oder, 19. Sprat, 21. Outcast, 22. Going for Gold.

Down: 1. Fixation, 2. Stage, 3. Scamp, 4. Sawmill, 5. Rind, 6. Amateurish, 7. Dehydrated, 11. Mel, 12. Fir, 13. Mediator, 14. Parting, 17. Goofy, 18. Storm, 20. Riot.

PUZZLE 53

Across: 1. Squaw, 4. Those, 10. Using, 11. Anguish, 12. Intrigue, 13. Kiri, 15. Mortal, 17. Forest, 19. Tame, 20. Lengthen, 23. Shadows, 24. Alvin, 25. Peggy, 26. Stack.

Down: 2. Quilt, 3. Anglican, 5. Huge, 6. Suicide, 7. Numismatist, 8. Hague, 9. Christening, 14. Poignant, 16. Rummage, 18. Mensa, 21. Havoc, 22. Song.

PUZZLE 57

Across: 1. Abysmal, 5. Dodd, 9. Strait, 10. Ellis, 12. Haydn, 13. Antique, 14. Rivers, 16. Cheers, 19. Erratic, 21. Starr, 23. Thong, 24. Unable, 25. Nosy, 26. Student.

Down: 2. Betty, 3. Shatner, 4. Astral, 8. Oblique, 7. Dispensary, 8. Heat, 11. Charleston, 15. Various, 17. Husband, 18. Acquit, 20. Togs, 22. Allan.

PUZZLE 50

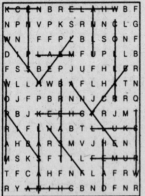

PUZZLE 54

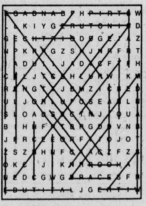

PUZZLE 58

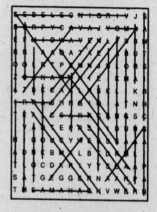

PUZZLE 51

Across: 1. Tawdry, 5. Lid, 7. Fairy, 8. Rebel, 9. Athlete, 13. Name, 14 Trent, 17. Scroll, 18. Fit, 19. Vigour, 20. Chant, 23. Eddy, 25. Layette, 28. Niece, 29. Lobby, 30. Tie, 31. Attend.

Down: 1. Turret, 2. Wobble, 3. Relent, 4. Wish, 5. Lyre, 6. Date, 7. Foam, 10. Test, 11. Larch, 12. Talon, 15. Raisa, 16. Noose, 18. Fret, 20. Cygnet, 21. Annexe, 22. Thread, 24. Dewy, 25. Left, 26. Yale, 27. Tube.

PUZZLE 55

Across: 1. Samuel, 7. Anecdote, 8. Remind, 9. Dote, 10. Luke, 12. Path, 14. Keen, 16. Royal, 18. Ember, 21. Chef, 24. Cher, 26. Alee, 27. Swan, 28. Guitar, 29. Disagree, 30. Rancid.

Down: 1. Shriek, 2. Mumble, 3. Ladder, 4. Vestry, 5. Sofia, 6. Peach, 11. Under, 12. Place, 13. Tone, 15. Etch, 17. Ode, 19. Beware, 20. Ranger, 22. Hectic, 23. Florid, 24. Crude, 25. Exist.

PUZZLE 59

Across: 1. Flack, 4. Churn, 10. Meryl, 11. Launder, 12. Eternity, 13. Bald, 15. Serial, 17. Priest, 19. Nick, 20. Commando, 23. Tourist, 24. Erica, 25. Jelly, 26. Bevel.

Down: 2. Lorre, 3. Calendar, 5. Haul, 6. Red tape, 7. Impersonate, 8. Bluto, 9. Traditional, 14. Premier, 16. Recluse, 18. Lofty, 21. Noise, 22. Pill.

PUZZLE 52

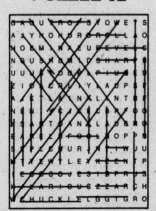

PUZZLE 56

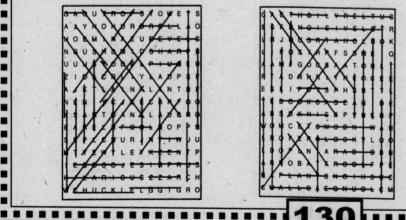

PUZZLE 60

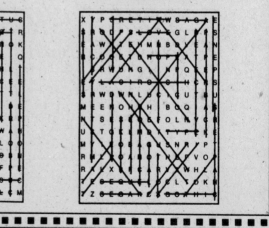

SOLUTIONS

PUZZLE 61

Across: 1. Displays, 5. Peep, 8. Mood, 9. Air force, 10 Appeals, 13. Rhine, 14. Leaf springs, 18. Borax, 19. Restore, 23. Carriers, 24. Bali, 25. Some, 26. Full moon.

Down: 1. Demean, 2. Scoop, 3. Avail, 4. Sure, 6. Ear-ring, 7. Peered, 11. Affix, 12. Super, 13. Reins, 15. Eardrum, 16. Abacus, 17. Legion, 20. Easel, 21. Otago, 22. Leaf.

PUZZLE 65

Across: 1. Raleigh, 7. Curio, 8. St. Leger, 9. Baxter, 11. Offal, 13. Pope, 14. Canasta, 15. Wife, 16. Basic, 17. Old Hat, 21. Deficit, 22. Salad, 23. Inferno. Down: 2. Artificial, 3. Elegance, 4. Gwen, 5. Puma, 6. Sift, 9. Blast, 10. Expedition, 12. Unfit, 13. Paradise, 18. Dray, 19. Arab, 20. Lean.

PUZZLE 69

Across: 1. Bantam, 4. Jackal, 7. Soar, 8. Limp, 10. Reins, 11. Twinkle, 14. Tee, 15. Token, 17. Tripe, 18. Dinah, 19. Lip, 21. Maestro, 24. Corfu, 26. Shop, 28. Moon, 29. Tinned, 30. Resume. Down: 1. Basket, 2. Throw, 3. Milan, 4. Jam, 5. Kwai, 6. Loosen, 9. Pretext, 11. Tern, 12. Isthmus, 13. Knife, 16. Kilo, 18. Decent, 20. Pounce, 22. Super, 23. Remus, 25. Rain, 27. Hod.

PUZZLE 62

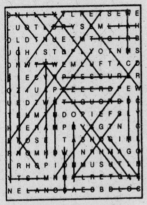

PUZZLE 66

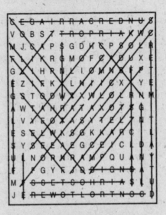

PUZZLE 70

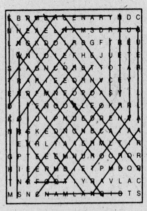

PUZZLE 63

Across: 1. Travel, 4. Willow, 7. Amin, 8. Gill, 9. Speech, 11. Fungi, 12. Tape, 14. Greta, 16. Catch, 18. Burma, 20. Tench, 21. Bess, 23. Ozone, 25. Angler, 28. Kiwi, 29. Silo, 30. Doctor, 31. Lounge. Down: 1. Traffic, 2. Align, 3. Loop, 4. Wore, 5. Light, 6. Wilde, 9. Sight, 10. Eternal, 13. Pam, 15. Abhor, 17. Ale, 19. Awesome, 21. Baked, 22. Saint, 24. Onion, 26. Gear, 27. Evil.

PUZZLE 67

Across: 1. Foolish, 5. Post, 7. Opal, 8. Islam, 9. Arid, 10. Aged, 12. York, 13. Degree, 17. Tutu, 18. Lei, 19. Long, 20. Senior, 24. Idea, 26. Rita, 27. Lint, 28. Poise, 29. Evel, 30. Bear, 31. Eyesore. Down: 1. Friend, 2. Oblong, 3. Inmate, 4. Honey, 5. Plankton, 6. Stiletto, 11. Doris, 14. Exorcise, 15. Register, 16. Elver, 21. Elapse, 22. Indigo, 23. Revere, 25. Aisle.

PUZZLE 71

Across: 1. Remote, 4. Scale, 7. Saw, 8. Segment, 9. Arrange, 10. Usher, 13. Tome, 14. Depart, 16. Via, 17. Clumsy, 20. Lift, 23. Spoon, 25. Approve, 26. Aniseed, 27. Ian, 28. Tread, 29. Crater. Down: 1. Resist, 2. Magnum, 3. Teeth, 4. Swerve, 5. Agenda, 6. Expect, 7. Star, 11. Seem, 12. Envy, 14. Damp, 15. Polo, 17. Chalet, 18. Umpire, 19. Stolid, 21. Invest, 22. Tinder, 23. Sean, 24. Osier.

PUZZLE 64

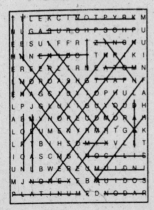

PUZZLE 68

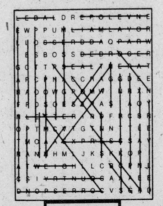

PUZZLE 72

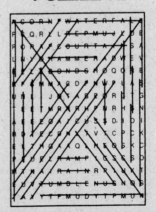

SOLUTIONS

PUZZLE 73

Across: 1. Fall out, 4. Marsh, 7. Work-out, 8. Hoard, 9. Embalm, 12. Aromatic, 15. Emma Wray, 17. Scream, 18. Mules, 21. Wart-hog, 22. Harry, 23. Gradual.
Down: 1. Florence, 2. Loofah, 3. Took, 4. Moth, 5. Royalty, 6. Hold, 10. Marry, 11. Powys, 13. Criminal, 14. Smaller, 16. Arnold, 18. Mash, 19. Sway, 20. Brig.

PUZZLE 77

Across: 1. Decorative, 8. Mansion, 9. Roger, 10. Oxen, 11. Lira, 12. Sat, 14. Tender, 15. Pippin, 18. Lop, 20. Digs, 21. Loni, 23. Tribe, 24. Trudeau, 25. Contraband.
Down: 1. Dungeon, 2. Chip, 3. Renoir, 4. Terrapin, 5. Vegas, 6. Immortaility, 7. Pretentious, 13. Dead heat, 16. Proceed, 17. Agatha, 19. Primo, 22. Pupa.

PUZZLE 81

Across: 1. Overlap, 5. Span, 9. Quince, 10. Least, 12. Outdo, 13. Harbour, 14. Assure, 16. Ethnic, 19. Chateau, 21. Passe, 23. Irked, 24. Ironic, 25. Tare, 26. Chianti.
Down: 2. Vault, 3. Rancour, 4. Aretha, 6. Platoon, 7. Nutcracker, 8. Slur, 11. Monarchist, 15. Slacker, 17. Tapioca, 18. Judith, 20. Ends, 22. Shift.

PUZZLE 74

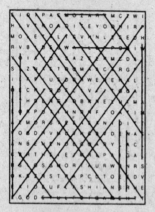

PUZZLE 78

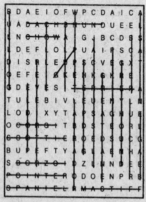

PUZZLE 82

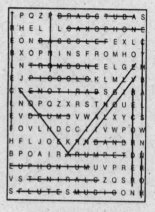

PUZZLE 75

Across: 1. Papoose, 7. Heron, 8. Stunned, 9. Cognac, 11. Grime, 13. Toll, 14. Nairobi, 15. Stet, 16. Vexed, 17. Artist, 21. Informs, 22. Sloop, 23. Antenna.
Down: 2. Alternator, 3. Ointment, 4. Seek, 5. Veto, 6. Worn, 9. Crook, 10. Able seaman, 12. Fight, 13. Tiresome, 18. Tale, 19. Soon, 20. Anon.

PUZZLE 79

Across: 1. Frost, 7. Disclose, 8. Banal, 10. Tournament, 12. Collapse, 14. Beer, 16. Jade, 17. Heptagon, 20. Evacuation, 23. Petal 24. Economic, 25. Stony.
Down: 1. Fabric, 2. Seat, 3. Pier, 4. Scrap, 5. Sovereign, 6. Jester, 9. Local, 11. Gladiator, 13. Sue, 15. Stoop, 16. Jeeves, 18. Newley, 19. Luxor, 21. Twin, 22. Newt.

PUZZLE 83

Across: 3. Obedience, 8. Hare, 9. Inflated, 10. Recall, 13. Crisp, 14. Furious, 15. Cod, 16. Example, 17. Badge, 21. Sextet, 22. Terminus, 23. Coda, 24. Battle-axe.
Down: 1. Character, 2. Practical, 4. Bails, 5. Defraud, 6. Egan, 7. Clef, 11. Toadstool 12. Essential, 14. Foe, 15. Cleanse, 18. Essex, 19. Deva, 20. Omit.

PUZZLE 76

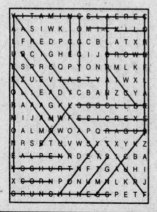

PUZZLE 80

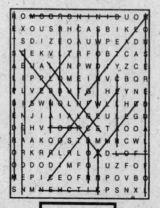

PUZZLE 84

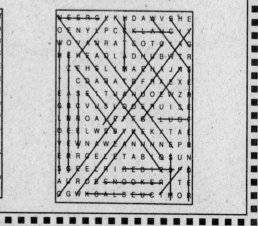

SOLUTIONS

PUZZLE 85

Across: 1. Reflect, 4. James, 7. Surmise, 8. Prise, 9. Shield, 12. Adequate, 15. Watching, 17. Handel, 18. Fifth, 21. Adapted, 22. Toddy, 23. Fertile.
Down: 1. Rickshaw, 2. Lauren, 3. Toil, 4. Jeep, 5. Magical, 6. Safe, 10. David, 11. Neagh, 13. Employee, 14. Stuffed, 16. Unrest, 18. Font, 19. Hazy, 20. Half.

PUZZLE 89

Across: 1. Polite, 5. Fat, 7. Loser, 8. Table, 9. Gudgeon, 13. Lion, 14. Large, 17. Invade, 18. But, 19. Ignite, 20. Flare, 23. Take, 25. General, 28. Brash, 29. Plans, 30. Bee, 31. Mellor.
Down: 1. Patrol, 2. Labour, 3. Treble, 4. Used, 5. Free, 6. Torn, 7. Logo, 10. Unit, 11. Gavel, 12. Order, 15. Argue, 16. Glide, 18. Beta, 20. Feeble, 21. Assail, 22. Either, 24. Alps, 25. Grab, 26. Nape, 27. Real.

PUZZLE 93

Across: 1. Punctual, 5. Bowl, 7. Lady, 8. Ignorant, 9. Centre, 12. Incline, 15. Yashmak, 19. Player, 21. Landmark, 22. Agog, 23. Wear, 24. Derelict.
Down: 1. Palace, 2. Crypt, 3. Unite, 4. London, 5. Burial, 6. Little, 10. News, 11. Roam, 12. Ink, 13. Coil, 14. I-spy, 15. Yellow, 16. Hinder, 17. Afraid, 18. Fright, 19. Poker, 20. Avail.

PUZZLE 86

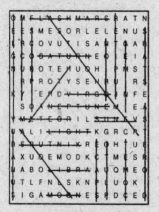

PUZZLE 90

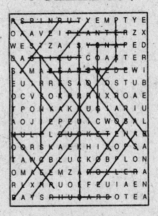

PUZZLE 94

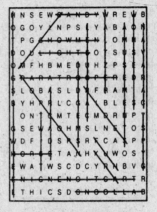

PUZZLE 87

Across: 1. Beef, 4. Slung, 7. Afloat, 8. Chow, 9. Ochre, 10. Cosmic, 11. Size, 12. Kapok, 13. Tilley, 16. Fort, 18. Ryan, 19. Dawdle, 21. Acute, 22. Bomb, 24. Leg-bye, 25. Crone, 26. Core, 27. Tragic, 28. Susie, 29. Aped.
Down: 1. Backs, 2. Fawcett, 3. Normal, 4. Stocky, 5. Unhappy, 6. Gherkin, 14. Lea, 15. End, 16. Francis, 17. Raucous, 18. Rebecca, 19. Delete, 20. Wigwam, 23. Blend.

PUZZLE 91

Across: 6. Congratulate, 8. America, 9. Punch, 10. Lava, 12. Beacon, 14. Caver, 15. Silver, 16. Mace, 19. Onset, 21. Origami, 22. Refrigerator.
Down: 1. Interval, 2. Grain, 3. Straw, 4. Slipper, 5. Stun, 6. Charleston, 7. Chandelier, 11. Jar, 12. Beg, 13. Chapatti, 14. Century, 17. Lodge, 18. Fibre, 20. Sled.

PUZZLE 95

Across: 6. Occasionally, 8. Patient, 9. Munch, 10. Exam, 12. Knight, 14. Tepee, 15. Sudden, 16. Tang, 19. Venom, 21. Primula, 22. Butterscotch.
Down: 1. Scotland, 2. Asset, 3. Mouth, 4. Jasmine, 5. Flan, 6. Oppressive, 7. Photograph, 11. Ben, 12. Keg, 13. Gratuity, 14. Termite, 17. Spare, 18. Witch, 20. Noun.

PUZZLE 88

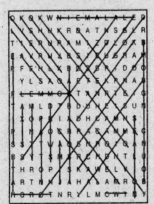

PUZZLE 92

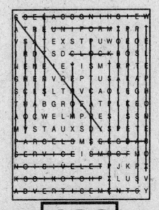

PUZZLE 96

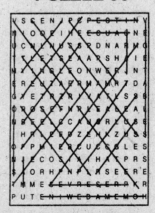

SOLUTIONS

PUZZLE 97

Across: 1. Voter, 5. Visor, 8. Ego, 9. Nudge, 10. Twice, 11. Span, 12. Heart, 15. Minute, 19. Each, 21. Rag, 22. Skin, 24. Endure, 28. Madoc, 31. Yap, 32. Swamp, 33. Odour, 34. Val, 35. Satan, 36. Essay.

Down: 1. Victim, 2. Titian, 3. Repent, 4. Month, 5. Vodka, 6. Siesta, 7. Riyadh, 13. Edge, 14. Read, 16. Ilk, 17. Ulna, 18. Ergo, 20. Car, 22. Stylus, 23. Import, 25. Nestle, 26. Uranus, 27. Employ, 29. Drown, 30. Curve.

PUZZLE 101

Across: 1. Service flat, 9. Integer, 10. Rotor, 11. Ribs, 12. Measured, 14. Defer, 15. Crisp, 20. Particle, 22. Irma, 24. Sabre, 25. Raiment, 26. Taken to task.

Down: 2. Eatable, 3. Vigo, 4. Career, 5. Forestry, 6. Actor, 7. Tiers, 8. pride, 13. Pekinses, 16. Sorters, 17. Spasm, 18. Claret, 19. Haste, 21. Rubia, 23. Diet.

PUZZLE 105

Across: 1. Capsicum, 5. Pits, 7. Rill, 8. Register, 9. Saddle, 12. General, 15. Phantom, 19. Lesser, 21. Contract, 22. Buck, 23. Year, 24. Electron.

Down: 1. Cerise, 2. Solid, 3. Carre, 4. Maggie, 5. Pestle, 6. Sorrel, 10. Dana, 11. Left, 12. Gum, 13. Nude, 14. Russ, 15. Plucky, 16. Nectar, 17. Ornate, 18. Broken, 19. Litre, 20. Sabot.

PUZZLE 98

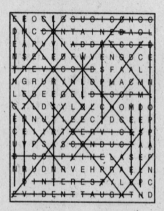

PUZZLE 102

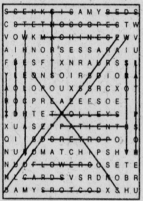

PUZZLE 106

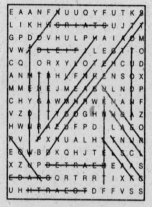

PUZZLE 99

Across: 1. Blush, 4. Adore, 10. Magma, 11. Leisure, 12. Relegate, 13. Dior, 15. Cereal, 17. Forget, 19. Task, 20. Graceful, 23. Othello, 24. Naive, 25. Spume, 26. Pinto.

Down: 2. Legal, 3. Shanghai, 5. Drip, 6. Rousing, 7. Imprecation, 8. Plate, 9. Deerstalker, 14. Tom Conti, 16. Rosehip, 18. Broom, 21. Flirt, 22. Plum.

PUZZLE 103

Across: 1. Valid, 4. Startle, 8. Roe, 9. Noble, 10. Amateur, 11. Sparse, 14. Tutor, 16. Dud, 18. Nausea, 19. Urchin, 21. Map, 22. Hound, 25. Emerge, 29. Lucille, 30. Gruff, 31. Ski, 32. Tornado, 33. Creel.

Down: 1. Venison, 2. Libra, 3. Dregs, 4. Seal, 5. Apart, 6. Treat, 7. Error, 12. Resin, 13. Edam, 15. Uncle, 17. Dupe, 20. Needful, 22. Holst, 23. Ulcer, 24. Delta, 26. Magic, 27. Route, 28. Peso.

PUZZLE 107

Across: 1. Playful, 5. Pupil, 8. Eva, 9. Sever, 10. Learn, 11. Rhyme, 12. Relay, 14. Terse, 15. Plot, 17. Dress, 20. Eject, 22. Cage, 23. Voice, 24. Aired, 27. Naked, 29. Litre, 30. Mogul, 31. Rap, 32. Enemy, 33. Totally.

Down: 1. Poser, 2. Anvil, 3. Ferry, 4. Levy, 5. Palette, 6. Prairie, 7. Lenient, 13. Err, 16. Leg, 17. Divulge, 18. Epistle, 19. Scenery, 21. Coe, 24. Admit, 25. Regal, 26. Dally, 28. Kept.

PUZZLE 100

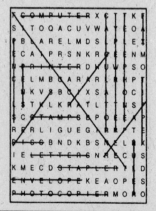

PUZZLE 104

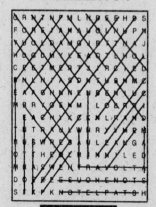

PUZZLE 108

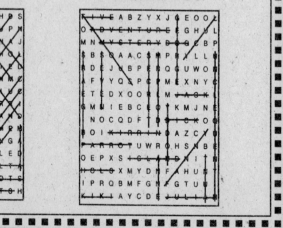

SOLUTIONS

PUZZLE 109

Across: 1. Clearly, 7. Cocoa, 8. Paddock, 9. Crafty, 11. Benny, 13. Amok, 14. Uranium, 15. Chum, 16. Tight, 17. Aplomb, 21. Satisfy, 22. Gourd, 23. Spindle.
Down: 2. Leadership, 3. Addendum, 4. Luck, 5. Boor, 6. Wolf, 9. Colin, 10. Thoughtful, 12. Jacob, 13. Ambition, 18. Leon, 19. Mark, 20. Harp.

PUZZLE 113

Across: 1. Persia, 5. Iran, 7. Drawn, 8. Tuna, 9. Hemp, 10. Prize, 11. Aspect, 13. Rory, 14. Halted, 18. Saturn, 21. Wasp, 22. Adrift, 24. Hones, 25. Sago, 26. Dojo, 27. Opted, 28. Pain, 29. Erects.
Down: 1. Pat Cash, 2. Spade, 3. Adapt, 4. Rations, 5. Inherit, 6. Admirer, 12. Cue, 15. Alabama,, 16. Typhoon, 17. Dignity, 19. And, 20. Nations, 22. Aside, 23. Ridge.

PUZZLE 117

Across: 1. Disorderly, 8. Banquet, 9. Panda, 10. Ewer, 11. Bell, 12. Axe, 14. Visual, 15. Lethal, 18. Tub, 20. Deft, 21. Bung, 23. Rough, 24. Agonise, 25. Respirator.
Down:1. Daniels, 2. Slug, 3. Rotter, 4. Espalier, 5. Linda, 6. Observatory, 7. Waterlogged, 13. Hardship, 16. Haulier, 17. Affarir, 19. Bruce, 22. Coat.

PUZZLE 110

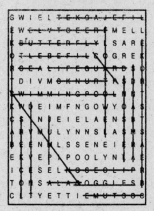

PUZZLE 114

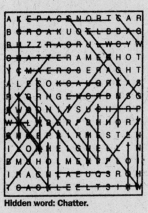

Hidden word: Chatter.

PUZZLE 118

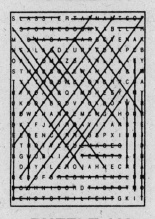

PUZZLE 111

Across: 6. Entrepreneur, 8. Trinklet, 9. Crete, 10. Need, 12. Trumps, 14. All in, 15. Untidy, 16. Inca, 19. Safer, 21. Marconi, 22. Conservative.
Down: 1. Strident, 2. Gecko, 3. Crate, 4. Unicorn, 5. Rule, 6. Extinguish, 7. Persuasive, 11. Ply, 12. Tim, 13. Mandolin, 14. Address, 17. Smirk, 18. Freak, 20. From.

PUZZLE 115

Across: 1. Benjamin, 5. Lens, 7. Throb, 8. Abscond, 9. Titillate, 13. Maya, 16. Via, 17. Dot, 18. YMCA, 21. Octagonal, 24. Cabinet, 26. Write, 27. Yarn, 28. Fearless.
Down: 1. Bothan, 2. Norway, 3. Abbot, 4. Nab, 5. Locality, 6. Sedge, 8. Apt, 10. Idaho, 11. India, 12. Talc, 14. Alec, 15. Aviation, 19. Marine, 20. Assess, 21. Orczy, 22. Nut, 23. Lower, 25. Elf.

PUZZLE 119

Across: 1. Product, 5. Whip, 9. Junior, 10. Allan, 12. Cleat, 13. Library, 14. Expire, 16. Sandal, 19. Episode, 21. Civic, 23. Abate, 24. Sluice, 25. Eyed, 26. Mystery.
Down: 2. Rouge, 3. Drifter, 4. Circle, 6. Holland, 7. Penny Black, 8. Lamb, 11. Accelerate, 15. Private, 17. Account, 18. Mersey, 20. Omen, 22. Vicar.

PUZZLE 112

PUZZLE 116

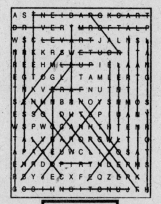

PUZZLE 120

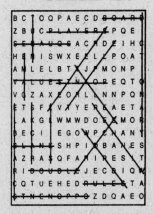

SOLUTIONS

PUZZLE 121

Across: 1. Archives, 5. Norm, 7. Halo, 8. Capacity, 9. Symbol, 12. Vacancy, 15. Complex, 19. Behave, 21. Theology, 22. Zero, 23. Hone, 24. Thriller.

Down: 1. Aghast, 2. H-Bomb, 3. Vocal, 4. Sophia, 5. Nicola, 6. Mayday, 10. Maim, 11. Oval, 12. Vex, 13. Cone, 14. NASA, 15, 15. Crutch, 16. Parole, 17. Effort, 18. Detour, 19. Buyer, 20. Hazel.

PUZZLE 125

Across: 1. Storage, 7. Litre, 8. Haggled, 9. Minute, 11. Spasm, 13. Gait, 14. Earlier, 15. Liar, 16. Syria, 17. Senior, 21. Musical, 22. Harry, 23. Bee Gees.

Down: 2. Trampoline, 3. Register, 4. Grey, 5. Kiri, 6. Urdu, 9. Minim, 10. Triplicate, 12. Pryor, 13. Grayling, 18. Neap, 19. Oars, 20. Lure.

PUZZLE 122

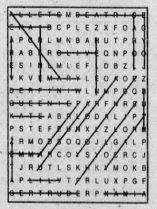

PUZZLE 123

Across: 1. Rabbit, 4. Debris, 7. Guru, 8. Teem, 10. Opera, 11. Shilton, 14. Tam, 15. Saved, 17. Plait, 18. Satyr, 19. Elm, 21. Emperor, 24. Perks, 26. Scar, 28. Even, 29. Rating, 30. Danger.

Down: 1. Regent, 2. Brush, 3. Total, 4. Die, 5. Rome, 6. Strand, 9. Monster, 11. Smut, 12. Impress, 13. Tramp, 16. Veer, 18. Supper, 20. Manner, 22. Erred, 23. Ocean, 25. Rust, 27. Cog.

PUZZLE 124

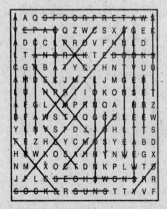